You are about to Enter A Book of Stories By a B-17 Pilot "Dewayne Bennett"

"When Shadows are
No Longer Cast in this Life,
I will Fly Away"

I dedicate this book to the 390th
Bomb Group Memorial Museum Foundation
And to my grandchildren

Ben
Megan
Jesse
Joe

Truth: Is It Really Stranger Than Fiction?

This little booklet came about after I had read the stories of various folks who flew in the 8th Air Force during WWII. Their chilling accounts of the adventures they underwent thrilled me to the bone, and I was prompted to write my own adventures. One pilot wrote about being upside down over Berlin with his bomb bay doors open, and the bombardier trying to salvo the bombs. The bombs fell through the roof and tore away the dingy (there are two in the roof of the plane) and left a gaping hole in the plane. Later when the ditched in the channel, they had no dingy and had to tie themselves together, inflate the Mae Wests, and hope the British Air Sea Rescue found them in time. Which they did.

My stories do not have the drama, terror, suspension, and horror of the average crew. We were the "Squawkin' Chicken," and the "Chicken Crew" destined to survive the horrible aspects of combat in the air. The Squawkin' Chicken nose art caused the German fighter pilots to laugh and point us out to other pilots. They would swoop past us, and we could see their oxygen masks shaking with laughter and pointing our nose art out to the others of the enemy. As a result we were never shot at. We never had a hole in our airplane, were never shot at, and with all the other planes crowding around us for protection. Scorned at first as cowards (the "Chicken Crew"), we were later recognized as a leader, with the other planes crowding around us so they wouldn't get shot up. It got so bad the group finally had to make us a lead crew, and we led the group about 15 times out of 31 missions.

When we first started flying combat, the other crews marked us as cowards (the "Chicken Crew"). When we left combat and finished our missions, we were the most popular crew to fly besides. You would not get shot at. When I came home, a friend wrote me and said there were 32 planes in the 8th Air Force named "The Squawkin' Chicken."

As you read this little book, remember these are the memories of an old man, married five times (now single), twice to the same woman, who has had a great time going through lo these many years. It has been real fun. And through it all, I have kept my sense of humor.

As you read, keep your tongue in cheek and a dish of peanuts to munch on. Grab a beer, or a glass of wine, and relive the adventures of an 82-year-old man who still thinks beautiful ladies (those over 79) are works of art and a joy to be with.

                                                  Yer Fren, Ben

Table of Contents

Spiced Meat & Potatoes

COMBAT TIME & LIFE OF SQUAWKIN' CHICKEN SKIPPER	7
BOMBER PILOT OR PLOW BOY	11
TRAINING FOR OVERSEAS	18
THE TOILET STOOL ACE	24
LUCKY	35

Raw Meat

THE STORY OF ASCEND CHARLIE	38
THE BAILEY CREW	46
LEGEND OF HEWITT (BUCK) DUNN	50
THE SHORT LIFE OF WILLIAM SEITZ	54
THE SETTLES CREW	59
BROTHERS	70
AIR SEA RESCUE MISSION	72
THE WINANT STORY	74
SLOW DOWN SMOKESTACK LEADER	77
SUMMARY	88
CREW DATA	91

BREWSTER
The Great Rooster

Stern of visage, steadfast, determined and dedicated to his flag, his country and his pullets. A symbol of glory, valor and bravery. "THE GREAT ROOSTER."

THE COMBAT LIFE AND
TIMES OF THE SQUAWKIN' CHICKEN SKIPPER

I was born in a tarpaper shack, on a hard scrabble, poor dirt farm in the middle of the United States. Iowa to be exact, in the south central part, not far from the Skunk River. The doctor arrived about 4 a.m., having been summoned by my grandfather. He had arrived in a Midwest thunder, lightening, and rainstorm. The rain had slashed at his old horse and buggy, and the top had not kept him from getting wet. He had taken a few nips of moonshine whiskey (called "Coal Miners' Fren") to help keep him warm and was staggering a bit when he arrived. My dad put the doctor's horse into the dry barn, and while they boiled water they drank coffee laced with some "Coal Miner's Fren." In the one-bedroom attached to the shack, my 18-year-old mother suffered her final labor pains. The thunder boomed; the lightening streaked the black sky; rain slammed against the windows; and the howling wind shook the old shack. In the kitchen the coal oil lamp gave off a soft light, the old wood-burning stove kept the coffee hot, and started the dishpan of water to steaming. My dad, the doctor (whom I will not name out of respect for his kin), and my grandpa slowly got drunk on the coffee and old "Coal Miner's Fren."

At about 5:30 a.m. on the rain- and wind-pounded morning of September 23, 1919, Edith Bennett (Nee Ansley) gave birth to an 8 pound, 21-inch baby boy. She wanted him named Dewayne Bennett (Dewayne from a romantic novel she had read), but the doctor on his shaking legs and in his quivering hand had written on the birth certificate Daine Bennett. (This was to cause me considerable trouble upon entering the service.) Afterwards, cleaned up, wrapped in a baby blanket, lying in my mother's arms I dozed half asleep, half awake, very happy to be here.

At about 6 a.m., the old rooster and his hens started waking up. The rooster, Old Watch, strutted out of the hen house and hopped up on a fence post. Facing the sun, he closed his eyes and let out a rip roaring "Cock-a-doodle-dooo," and again, "Cock-a-doodle-dooo!" In the quiet of the country morning, the sound reverberated across the yard and penetrated the bedroom of the little shack. My mother slept through the "Cock-a-doodle-dooo" cry, but they say the little baby (me) instantly came alert, his eyes crossed, his tongue hung out as he tried to imitate, or answer the call of the "Great Rooster." It was to affect my whole life. I would never be the same, and many years later a famous psychiatrist was to explain that I had been infected with what is called "THE CHICKEN SYNDROME." It was from hearing the call of the "Great Rooster" both in the womb, and on that early morning of September 23, 1919. It all began that early morning with the warm sun rising over the rain-soaked landscape. To this day, when I see a chicken spread its wings I get the urge to fly again myself.

My early life was filled with happy memories. Going to school in a one-room country school, walking the long distance in the fall when the leaves were changing color and falling, and walking through the cold and snow during the winter, and then the beautiful beginning of spring. I have memories of visiting my grandmother and grandfather, spending the night in their one-bedroom weather-beaten house with the big pot-bellied stove in the front room. They lived in a small town of about 450 people, and they knew everyone in town.

My grandfather had two mules, Prince and Nellie. Prince was a blue mule with white hair sprinkled into the blue, a beautiful coat. He had been a mule that worked in the coal mines in Iowa. He had spent so much time in the dark tunnels that he was almost blind. He had taken ill in the mine and rather than let him die there they brought him out. He had recovered, and when they tried to take him back he raised so much hell they sold him to my grandfather. Nellie was a big old yellow mule, cantankerous and mean, but she and Prince got along great. They worked well together with the light hauls my grandfather contracted for in the small town. He hauled a load of coal now and then moved families, hauled lumber and ties for the railroad. All the light hauls he did into his eighties.

On the farm we had two teams. One team was a young team of mules, Tom and Jerry, who my dad was training to work together as a team. They were blue Missouri mules like Prince in color, but they were young and hard to train. Blaze and Dot were mother and daughter, huge farm animals, reddish brown in color with black manes and tails. They both had a white streak down their faces. They did all the hard work, were gentle, and fun to be around.

I went to country school through the eighth grade and one year in town through the ninth grade. That was the extent of my education, and being big for my age, went to work on the farm. My life revolved around the two mules, Tom and Jerry. Long hours in the sun with a hand plow, then breaking up the clods with a harrow, and then hours spent planting corn. We had a wire with knots on it. This was stretched from one end of the field to the other, and the knots tripped the corn planter. Every row had to be straight in every direction, and the distance between the rows uniform.

By this time, you are asking, what does this have to do with flying? Let me explain. I spent hours looking at those mule rear ends and finally got to noticing what direction the tail was pointing. If it was slightly to the right, I knew we were in a right turn. Similarly, when to the left, we were in a left turn. Straight down, we were going straight. This was an amazing discovery, and one that was to stand me in good stead when I got in an airplane and stated flying blind. Flying blind meant you had to trust the instruments, and the needle ball was a friendly and familiar instrument for me. I just imagined that it was a mule's tail upside down. It was amazing and I was a natural born instrument pilot.

War clouds loomed on the horizon. The draft was put into effect, and farmers were ruled essential to the war effort. My draft number was high and I told my dad, "Don't worry, they will never take me. My number is too high."

Ben Speaketh

BOMBER PILOT or PLOW BOY

I was born near Lovilla, Iowa, Sept 23, 1919, and that's a fact. My Mother was 18 years old and my dad was 24. I spent the next 21 years of my life on the farm, and a great deal of that time was spent behind a team of Missouri mules. I learned a lot about them and they learned a lot about me.

Mules never learned to like anybody. They would do their work with a minimum of effort, then expected to be fed and watered. They had more stamina than a horse and conserved their energy, they were smart, but would kick the hell out of you if they got a chance. They were fractious, mean and ornery, but they worked hard, in the hot Iowa summer sun, pulling a turning plow acre after acre. I spent many hours alone with them. Tom and Jerry was the last team I worked before going into the Air Force, and I always attributed my success as a pilot to those mules. They were big Missouri mules, colored sort of bluish gray with white hair sprinkled through their coat. They were handsome mules, and I spent much time running a currycomb over their sleek coats. I was proud of them and liked to show them off.

I was tall, weighed about 200 pounds, and was in good shape from all the walking, lifting, pulling, and straining from farm work. We didn't have tractors, and everything was done with a team of horses or mules, and by hand. We put up barbed wire fencing, and cut our own posts from timber on the river bottom. We butchered our own meat, usually killing a hog when it got a little cold in the fall. We cut and stacked hay, planted corn in the spring and picked it in the fall, and always after dark, milked 14 cows.

There was no electricity or refrigeration so the hogs we butchered had to be cut up, fried into sausage, salted down or frozen outside. We dressed in overalls, usually with no shirt, and the big brogans for foot wear. In the wintertime we wore long handled underwear, and almost every male farmer in Iowa wore a sheepskin coat bought out of the Sears and Roebuck catalog. I didn't have a white shirt or dress pants until I was 21 years old and always felt self-conscious when I had to put them on.

In 1940 war clouds were forming, and the martial music was playing with lots of drum rolls and occasionally "Taps" was heard on the radio (by this time we had electricity). Occasionally President Roosevelt would have a "fireside chat," and about the draft. I wasn't too worried about being drafted, because farming was a critical occupation, and the draft board classified me as essential to the war effort. After December 7, 1941 things started to change. My draft number was 852, and I told my dad, "Don't worry, my number is so high they will never get to me."

In Washington DC Secretary of War Stimpson put on one of those high silk hats, a frock coat, goin' to a wedding pants, and new patent leather shoes. In front of the Newsreel cameras he reached into a little fish bowl, and the first draft number he pulled out was 22. The second was 852. My draft exemption was canceled, and ten days later I was down at the courthouse for my physical.

Flying an airplane in the pre-war Army Air Corp was considered so important and difficult that only West Pointers were allowed to do it. These fellows were educated at West Point. They had to be perfect specimens. They had all their teeth, their features had to be perfect. So many hairs on their head, and the ears had to lie close to the head at an angle of not more than 10 degrees. The pupils of their eyes must be 2 3/4 inches apart, no bags under the eyes, and the head had to be round and well framed; no pinheads were allowed. They were highly educated in English, military history, mathematics, and discipline. They were also taught the social graces, and above all taught to be gentlemen. The term, "Officer and a gentleman," were common in the service.

The military planners had figured out that getting a bomb on the target was going to be a difficult proposition. The pilot had to hold the plane straight and level for the bomb aimer to get the bombs on the target. It was determined that the pilot would have to hold the plane straight and level for at least 10 minutes. In that 10 minutes every gun the enemy had would be aimed at the airplane. There would be much shot and shell, gnashing of teeth, strife and bloodshed; there was no way to estimate the losses. The truth was, there would be losses, and many of them would be pilots. Rank, education, station in life, officer and a gentleman didn't make a bit of difference. A bullet didn't recognize an officer from an enlisted man.

When word reached all of the West Point pilots there was consternation. "We're the leaders," they said to one another. "It seems foolhardy to send the leaders into such a nightmarish situation." It would be dangerous to run the risk of decimating the leadership ranks, the highly educated upper echelon officers (West Pointers), and have them fly that extremely dangerous 10 minute bomb run.

After much discussion, it was decided to have a study done, by a group of high level professors. Their mission was to find out what type of American youth was dumb enough to set in that big airplane for a ten long minutes on the bomb run. They would be like ducks in a shooting gallery, while everybody shot at them with every conceivable type of weapon intending to kill or maim him. They engaged professors from Yale, Harvard, Princeton, Columbia, Cornell, and Penn State.

They met during the day and debated the qualifications of various groups of young men. They eliminated lawyers immediately, knowing they were too highly educated to participate in a dumb thing like flying straight and level for 10 minutes while the enemy shot at you. They argued pro and con the merits of college educated against high school educated young men. They debated for days, and weeks that it took a highly educated young man to fly the mighty Flying Fortress, or the Liberator heavy bombers. After all, up to this time, only the highly educated West Pointers had been allowed to fly in the Army Air Corp.

They struggled with the question of "Who would be dumb enough to get in the cockpit of a heavy bomber, and fly straight and level for ten minutes on the Bomb run? After much sweating, straining, and soul searching, and much disagreement among themselves, they came up with a report. They were more than happy that they had found a small group of people in the United States who fit the criteria. The only enigma in the whole report was that if this classification of folks were dumb enough to fly the bomb run, were they so dumb they couldn't be taught to fly? The professors threw up their hands on this question, they had all gained weight (eating the Waldorf Astoria cooking) they were tired and wanted to go home.

Let the Army Air Corp figure that one out they reasoned, as they filled out the report, signed it, and handed it to the General in charge. The professors scooted for home happy that they had done their duty for humanity and their country. The money didn't matter after all it was for their country.

Five Generals, two Colonels, three Lieutenant Colonels, one Second Lieutenant, and a private (their names are not important) were present when the report was opened. It was fill of therefore, whereas, henceforth and other related report gibberish, but it boiled down to this:
"Don't get city slickers to do this }ob. They are too smart to set 10 minutes in a heavy bomber, loaded with 2800 gallons of gasoline, ten 500 pound bombs, 7000 rounds of 50 caliber ammunition, with an aluminum skin that burns with searing hot flames at the drop of a kitchen match. They will manage to evade this duty and it will all be legal. Which leaves the only individuals, that in our opinion, fulfills all categories of the requirement, the dumb old farm boys from the farm states. The dumbest ones of all are those with a ninth grade

education whose occupation was driving a team of mules plowing straight furrows for a cornfield Therefore we suggest you code name your endeavor "Plowboy" and seek out at least 5000 of them for test over enemy targets. "

Immediately orders went out to recruiting stations all over the United States to: *"Direct your attention, and watch carefully for young men with plow boy experience, particularly those who worked behind a team of mules, or were mule skinners, and had little formal education. Commanders are ordered to survey your ranks for personal in the above category, and hurry them into the Aviation Cadet program. The code name for this operation will herein after be labeled "PLOWBOY."*

The 'Plow Boy' program was given top priority in recruiting requirements, with the stipulation, *'Make it without undue speed or excitement for them to enlist, but with a confident certainty that they will enlist."* Thus, the die was cast and plowboys become a valuable commodity in the recruiting wars.

With a ten-day notice to report for induction, I put on a clean shirt, and headed to Des Moines. I took a bus to the federal building where the recruiting office was located, and marched right in. A Master Sergeant was behind the desk. He was writing on a piece of paper, and didn't look up. I was standing in front of the desk, and took to fidgeting, and scuffling my feet after about ten minutes of this inattention. Finally he looked up at me, and in a disgusted voice said, "Whaddya' want?" "Well sir, I'd sure like to enlist in the United States Army Air Corp, and be a pilot."

I was dressed in my overalls, a clean work shirt, and my big brogan shoes, and he looked me up and down before answering, "What the hell makes you think you're fit to be a pilot in the United States Army Air Corp. you sure don't look like much." "Well Sir," I responded getting mildly angry, "I think I have all the smarts to be a good pilot, and I can read and write."

He looked at me in amazement, "You need two years of college or you have to pass a college equivalency test. Do you think you can do that? '

I was on the defensive now, "Well, I'd sure like to try." He sensed he was trapping me, "How much education do you have?" He was scowling as he asked me that. "Well Sir, I finished the ninth grade."
"He slapped his palm to his forehead, and in exasperation said, "you need a hell of a lot more education than a ninth grade education.
What kind of work did you do?" "Well Sir," I said, "I was a farmer and plowed with a team of mules. We had to plow straight furrows, and my mules were named Tom and Jerry. You might say that I was a PLOWBOY."

There was the worst clatter and banging as a chair was turned over in the office next to the recruiting office. An officer came charging through the door. He exploded at the Sergeant, "I don't want to ever hear you talk to our future pilots like that again, and if any more of these PLOWBOYS come in here I want to be notified at once."
The Sergeant responded with a meek, "Yes sir."

Taking me by the arm the Second Lieutenant ushered me into his office, offered me a seat, which I took, and a cigarette which I declined. He shook hands with me twice, telling me how happy he was to see me. He asked my name, straightened up his chair, and sat down facing me. He was smiling from ear to ear, as he pulled out some papers from the middle desk drawer of his desk. He then proceeded to tell me about the order he had just received in the mail from his superiors telling him to sign up PLOWBOYS. "Just put your name, date of birth, and your address on this paper, and sign it," he was smiling.

I took the paper and did as he directed, and signed it. He grabbed the paper scribbled his signature on the bottom. He told me I didn't have to take a physical, no college equivalency tests, and all I had to do was show up for the train when they shipped us to Santa Ana for our initial training.

I was feeling pretty good about being a pilot, and he reached in the middle drawer, pulled out a big rubber stamp, and slammed it down on the paper I had just signed. To this day, I DON'T KNOW WHETHER IT READ "BP" FOR BOMBER PILOT OR "PB" FOR PLOWBOY.

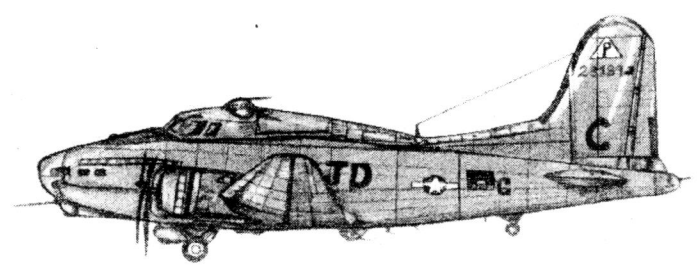

TRAINING AND OVERSEAS

There were ten members on the crew. We were all young. One member 18 years old, and one 19 years old. The rest 20 to 24 years of age. They were from New York City, Ada, Oklahoma, Los Angeles, California, Antigo, Wisconsin, and several right off the farm just like me. I had been a PLOWBOY, living on a farm, in Iowa, working behind a team of mules (Tom and Jerry) now thrust into a situation, with only a ninth grade education, to making sure that the nine young men placed in my charge would make it home. It was a hell of a responsibility, and caused me sleepless nights, and much anxiety. I knew some of their families. They jumped into that B-17 sure in their minds that the co-pilot and me would get them there and bring them back. I used to look at them and wonder how they had such confidence in their pilot and co-pilot. I was fresh out of B-17 transition school, and was not really comfortable in the cockpit, and really sweated out the landings. I never got the knack of looking sharp in the uniform. My shirt tail was usually out, and my pants baggy at the knees. The only item I was comfortable with was the big brogan shoes. I had worn them all my life on the farm, but we sure as hell didn't spit shine them.

The Army Air Force wanted all your clothes knife edge sharp. They wanted sharply pressed pants, and the shirt was supposed to have three creases in the back, and two in the front. However, the worst problem I had was with the tie. I had never worn a tie. I had never tied a tie. The knot was a total mystery to me. I had the co-pilot tie one for me and I just slipped it over my head. I finally had one tied and took it to a lady in Roswell, NM who cut the band and put in a button hole and button. It may have been the first clip on tie in history, but it worked. I was often reprimanded for inappropriate dress, but, hell I noticed a couple other old plowboys looked just like me. Remember we plowboys were in the service, on the PLOWBOY Recruitment Program, and they couldn't do any thing to us. One of the pilots I mention had only an eighth grade education, and came into the same group I did. The 384th Bomb Group, and became the most highly decorated member of our Group. He won the Distinguished Service Cross, The Silver Star, and the Purple Head. When he went before the General to receive the Distinguished Service Cross, his shirt tail was out, his pants not pressed and his tie was improperly knotted. The other plowboy mentioned was killed in May of 1944 with the 92nd Bomb Group. There was no mention of his uniform in his death notice.

At Dalhart AAB, Texas, we learned to fly formation, took long cross countries, for navigational training (alone) all over the United States. We simulated making bomb runs on the cities, Los Angeles, Denver, Dallas, New Orleans, and most of it was done at night. This was before urban sprawl, and the towns dotted the beautiful United States each an individual group of lights, not run together like now days. We graduated from Dalhart in February of 1944. There was a graduation ceremony held in the Gymnasium, However, the three PLOWBOY pilots, and their crews were not invited to the ceremonies. Our certificates were given to us along with our orders to report to Kearny AAFB, Nebraska.

When we got to Kearney, Neb, The PLOWBOY crews were advised that we would probably just get on a B-17 and ride to England with better pilots. After the first night it was obvious that some of the pilots had got lost with their crews, through snowstorms, rain storms, troop trains breaking down, and some of them in hospitals.

They were missing five crews. As a result the PLOWBOY crews were hurried into service, briefed, put in a new airplanes and told to go to Manchester, NH.

On February 24, 1944 we picked up B-17G number *43-97150* in Kearney, Nebraska. There was a bill of lading in the seat of this brand new airplane that said the value was $198,000. Having come from a poor farm family, and never seen more than $200.00 in one chunk, I was overwhelmed. I had to sign for the $198.000 airplane, and we departed at 2:40 AM bound for the air war in Europe.

Early in the morning I refused to let the co-pilot go down and buzz his father's farm. He was a little upset with me We had a new navigator, Aldo Rovero, and I kept him busy answering questions as to where we were. I wasn't about to go down and buzz a farm in the early morning light, and continued to fly by the book. The co-pilot later became a first pilot, and when the responsibility of the crew weighted on him, he understood my reluctance to let him buzz his dad's farm. We landed at Manchester, NH at 11:30 AM. We were confined to the base and were ordered to prepare for take off the next morning for Goose Bay, Labrador.

I'm not sure what time the crew was to report to the airplane, but everyone did except fur the waist gunner Kenneth Wyatt. Wyatt was a very young man, 18 or 19 years old from Los Angeles, California He had gotten married while we were still in training. He kept us waiting for over an hour, and I had asked for a jeep to try and find him. Just as I was ready to leave he came ambling up. I ordered him on the airplane and must confess I really chewed his ass. Fifty years later, and after he was dead, I know I should have left him that day, and picked up another waist gunner in England He had an obsession that he would be shot down, and sure enough he went down with another crew, and became a POW.

As we headed for Goose Bay, Labrador the weather got progressively worse. We climbed to get over the clouds and when we arrived over Goose Bay we were at 33,000 feet (the highest I ever got in a B-17) and were skimming the tops of the clouds. Goose Bay Tower advised they were closing the field, and sent us back to Presque Isle, Maine and we arrived there at 1830 (6:30 PM).

The weather cleared on March 3, 1944 and we flew from Presque Isle, Maine to Goose Bay, Labrador, arriving at 1400 (2:00 PM) with a total flying time of five hours.

There was deep snow at Goose Bay. Snow was piled up along the runway about 4 or 5 feet deep. As soon as we landed heaters were put on the engines. We ate and were told to get some sleep. The three PLOWBOY crews were told that we would be flown across the Atlantic by three. We then reduced power, and leaned the engines out as much as we dared. Through the night and early morning we slowly descended and finally broke out with scattered clouds below us at about 12,000 feet.

During the night Aldo Rovero, the navigator, had asked me to make a rather drastic course change. I questioned him, but not knowing myself where we were I made the change. Below we could see the white caps, and to go down in that frigid water meant certain death even if you survived the crash. But the engines sang a beautiful song without a skip or a beat. I was tired, felt like Lucky Lindy Lindburgh (he flew the Atlantic alone in 1927). And we landed at Meeks Field in Iceland at noon (1200 hours) just as Rovero had estimated. I never doubted him again and he became a lead navigator in the 384th Bomb Group.

It was a cold barren landscape, and a bitter wind was blowing and not a tree in sight. The supply ship was late and food was scarce and we had powdered eggs and toast for dinner, and again for breakfast. We spent the night here and took off for Scotland the next day.

We took off from Meeks Field Iceland at 8:30 AM and had an uneventful flight to Preswick, Scotland, landing at 1330 with a total flying time of 5 hours. We were impressed with the beautiful green landscape we were flying over in Scotland. It was a sea of green, grass and frees; one of the things that has been attached to my memory lo these many yearn.

They took our airplane, 42-97150 away. She had carried us safely from Kearney, Nebraska to Preswick, Scotland. Everything worked without a hitch which I can't say for seventeen out of the twenty in our group that left Keamey. When I went to debriefing there were two other pilots from our group there. You guessed it, the other two PLOWBOYS had made it along with me. The three old PLOWBOYS who were supposed to be flown over the great Atlantic Ocean by experienced pilots had done it all by our own selves. It took about two weeks for all seventeen of the other planes **to** get into Preswick. The three old PLOWBOYS, with their shirt tails out, un-pressed pants, no spit shine on the GI brogans, no stiff straight posture had made it on time. We had already been assigned to Combat Bombardment Groups by the time the rest of them got to

Preswick. I and one other PLOWBOY were assigned to the 384th Bombardment Group, and the other was assigned to the 92nd Bombardment Group.

On March 24, 1944 our crew arrived at the 384th Bombardment Group, and were assigned to the 545th Bombardment Squadron. When we went to our barracks and entered there were a few men setting around a little stove playing poker. We tried to strike up a conversation, but they were rather abrupt. When we asked which bed we could take one of them said, "Take any empty one, they won't be back. It was a chilly greeting.

The history of B-17 42-97150 is as follows: 42-97150, 547th Squadron, SO-F, 544th Squadron SU-F, named "SILVER QUEEN" was accepted by the Air Force February 2, 1944, and flown overseas February 3, 1944. She was assigned **to** the 384th Bombardment Group on March 12, 1944. On September 16 she was sent to the Air Force Service Command, and returned to the Group October 10, 1944. On January 19, 1945 she landed on the continent, and failed to return to the base. She was salvaged (junked) where she landed.

THE
TOILET STOOL ACE

Americans are an ingenious lot. They look for ways to do things better and easier. Some might construe that Americans are lazy, but I like to think it's common sense, learned through years of hard won freedom. Freedom to think and a strong entrepreneurial streak in their makeup that wants to improve on any project that needs to be improved upon. Give an American a nail, hammer and a piece of bailing wire, and watch out, he's liable to improve a procedure, or piece of equipment that has been in use for a thousand years.

I'm talking about a period of time before and during WW I, up to and through the 50s. Modem educational methods had not yet taken hold, and when the public schools still educated young people. I ended up with a ninth grade education, came right off the farm, and became a heavy bomber pilot in the US Army Air Corps (how I got in the U. S. Army Air Corps is another story). At Douglas, Az. Army Air Force Base in August of 1943, they put the Second Lieutenant's bars on my shirt collar and shoulders.

I was a commissioned officer and a gentleman according to the standards off the US Army. I was also a good candidate for a POW or little tag after my name on some unknown list in the future. It was inevitable that I was bound for a foreign shore to fight the enemy, Germany or Japan, and no matter how I schemed, malingered, vacillated, or just plain screwed off my destiny was assured. I was an Old Plowboy, and I was headed for Combat.

After I got my 2nd Lt.'s bars and wing's they gave me a 10-day leave, and I reported to Roswell Army Air Force Base in Roswell, New Mexico for transition into the B- 17, The Flying Fortress. She was loaded with gun turrets, radios, switches and dials, and huge gasoline tanks. I could imagine when you loaded this thing with 2800 gallons of high octane gasoline, thousands of rounds of 50 caliber machine gun bullets, and five thousand pounds of high explosive bombs, and you were setting in the pilot's seat (which is where I'd be sitting) your ass was in great danger. It looked to me like a risky, dangerous business, and I asked if I could be transfer to cooking school. However, they said there was more applications from pilots than there was openings.

I finished up at Roswell, learned to fly that big Flying Fortress (I never did learn to start the engines, but that's another story), and was sent to Salt Lake City to pick up a crew. They were all extremely young men, who looked at me with questioning eyes, "Can that stupid looking Plowboy fly that big Flying Fortress?" I did my best to look professional and to assure them that I was a competent pilot, and no longer a corn picker. To this day I wonder if I succeeded.

We boarded a troop train in Salt Lake City, and meandered down through Colorado to the little town of Dalhart, Texas. Dalhart is in the panhandle of Texas, and is flat prairie grasslands with some big ranches, little towns, and blizzards like I had never seen before. In the cowboy books I had read as a kid the cowboys had dreaded the "blue northers", and I can understand why. There were a thousand pictures with the cowboy in the wind driven snow with a calf draped over the saddle.

I came to dread that winter in Dalhart, the snow blowing and the howling wind.. We were housed in primitive Quonset huts with a pot-bellied stove that burned wood or coal. It was tough getting up in the early morning and starting a fire, especially if the flap of your long winter underwear had accidentally unbuttoned in a restless nightmare (usually B-17s crashing in flames with the pilot still strapped in the seat) filled sleep.

There was no let up in the training. The air war in Europe was heating up and the 8th Air Force had lost 60 bombers on one day in October of 1943. It was hailed as a great victory for the U. S. Army Air Forces, but the requests to transfer to cooking school went up dramatically among the future combat pilots.

We were now a combat crew. We were through with training, ready to go and fight the Hun. I can't say we were rearm' to go, but we were on our way. They issued us a new airplane, jungle packs, and sent us on our way from Kearney, Nebraska. We were to fly from Kearney to Manchester, N.H., to Goose Bay, Labrador, Iceland, Scotland, and then England.

It was a sweat flying over the forbidding, wind whipped Atlantic Ocean, looking down from 20,000 feet it looked bone chilling cold, and certain death to fall into it's clutches.

We were assigned to the 384th Bombardment Group, 545th Squadron, at Grafton Underwood, England. We were a new crew, the first one into this squadron, in some time and no one went out of their way to welcome us. I flew a couple of missions as a co-pilot, and on our first mission as a crew all of the old crews in our squadron were shot down. They brought in three crews with experience (10 missions or more) and three new crews to fill out the squadron. Two weeks later our squadron lost the three experienced crews, including the Squadron Commander, Captain Langlois, and I was the most experienced pilot in the Squadron with six missions.

One of the tactics used by the German fighter pilots against heavy bombers was mind-blowing and murderous. Our crews considered it un-sportsman like and down right dirty. We had seen several B-17s go down from this dastardly maneuver, and had been thinking and talking about ways to sting the Hun when he tried it on us. The German fighter would circle the formation paying particular attention to the ball turret gunners. They were hoping to find a plane with the turret inoperative, out of ammunition, or maybe with the gunner wounded and out of the turret. Finding his prey with an inoperative turret, the Hun would snake his way up under the wounded B-17, pull up sharply, hanging the fighter on the prop, and pour deadly 20mm fire into the unprotected belly. When the B-17 blew up, the fighter would fall off and dive straight down. The Germans called it, "Der unterbelly caper." This incensed our crew, and we scratched our heads trying to come up with a method that would protect the underbelly even though the ball turret was inoperative.

We had ideas about dropping a large hook, attached to a cable,. and try to snare the fighter. We thought about dropping chains into the prop, but nobody would volunteer to stand on the bomb bay catwalk and drop the chains at the right time. It was difficult to get anyone to stand in the frigid cold bomb bay with the doors open, and the wind and air stream shrieking and howling like a wounded banshee. Especially at 20,000 or 25,000 feet, then it was downright terrorizing with the bomb bay doors open.

One crewman suggested we drop used engine oil on the fighter thereby fouling up his windshield, and if he couldn't see he couldn't fire, but how do we get the stuff on the hun's airplane?

The latter suggestion straightened out our thinking, and we came up with the jellied gasoline idea. It was known at that time that oil-drilling mud (Bentonite) would gel gasoline. Could we rig up a five-gallon can of jellied gasoline, hinged in the bomb bay with a bailing wire running into the cockpit so the pilot could dump the can on command? The ball turret gunner could fire into the gob of jellied gasoline with 50-caliber tracer ammunition, and it would burn the fighter just before he started shooting. It was a bodacious idea; it was doable, and we were setting around congratulating ourselves for a great idea.

Our first test came on a mission to Berlin, May 7, 1944. The weather was marginal, but we got through to the target and dropped our bombs. The five-gallon can rested in the bomb bay undisturbed, but not for long. Several Me-109s came sniffing around the formation so we told the ball turret gunner to track the fighters but not to fire. Sure enough one of the fighters started ducking in and out to see if the ball turret gunner was going to shoot at him. We held off, until suddenly he was below us pulling up to hang on his prop. When the gunner yelled, "Now!," I pulled the wire and the jellied gasoline went out. In one big gob. The slipstream tore the gob apart, but some of it hit the fighter's windshield, and he was startled by the mass coming at him. He fell into a dive without firing.

We were disappointed by our lack of success, but not discouraged. We increased the Bentonite on the next try, and put in a quart of sorghum that my Grandmother had sent me. The results out of a five-gallon can were again unsuccessful, and we came back from Saarbrucken, Germany on May 11, 1944, a mighty unhappy crew.

We had managed to set this gob on fire, but it was so scattered that it did no harm to the fighter. It scared the hell out of the pilot of the fighter; he thought the B-17 had exploded and was coming down on him.

Now then, here's where American ingenuity comes into the picture. This is what I was talking about at the beginning of this article. A young man, hardly 20 years old, and one of the waist gunners, we'll call him Verlin, came to me, and said he had an idea about dropping the gobs of jellied gasoline. He told me he was hesitant to make the suggestion for fear the rest of the crew would laugh at him."I think I've figured out a way to drop that jellied gasoline in one big gob," he said, "but I'm afraid everyone in the crew will laugh." "Well, what the hell, if it's a good idea we'll try it. We sure need to improve on that five-gallon can," I replied. "Well, I got the idea setting on the crapper," he hesitated. "Go on," I urged.

"When I flushed the stool I noticed that the water rushed out of the tank into the bowl, and it swirled and fell out of the bowl in a mass. If we could rig up a toilet stool in the bomb bay, close to the bottom of the plane it would fall in a gob. In addition if we could drop it slightly before the fighter pulled up the gob would travel with the speed of our plane, and fall in a curve. Don't you see Sir, it would be just like a bomb falling out of the bomb bay only our target would be closer." He was animated and his face was flushed wit excitement. "If our mixture was just right the gob would spread like a blanket, and engulf the whole fighter plane."

I was excited, as dumb as it sounded the logic behind the idea had merit. It warranted a trial run. I told him to get the rest of the crew and start hunting up a toilet stool and tank. My actual orders to him were, "Find a stool, and I won't ask any questions."

I went to work with a five-gallon can mixing the gasoline and the bentonite, until the mixture was right, and then added another quart of my Grandma's sorghum. We put the sorghum in the mixture to make it sticky, and by the time I had stirred all that sorghum in our mixture was fluid but sticky. We thought about mixing in a quart of peanut butter, but that would have made it so thick and sticky it wouldn't flush. We made copious notes of our mixture so we could duplicate it.

By this time the crew had returned with a toilet stool complete with a tank. They had thoughtfully covered it with a canvas tarp. I really wasn't anxious to have the crew chiefs know what we were doing to their airplane. I certainly didn't want the other crews knowing and damn sure didn't want the commanding officer to know. He probably would have taken a dim view of out idea. While we were mounting the toilet in the bomb bay my crew started calling me Captain Sticky; that name stuck to me for sometime.

After we had the toilet mounted, and the bailing wire was threaded to the cockpit, we notified the crew chief what we had done, and asked him to keep quiet about it. Because I was the senior pilot in the squadron, he said it was OK, and was anxious to know how it worked. After a while he started calling me Captain Sticky.

The big day for the test came on May 13, 1944; a mission to Stettin, Germany. Stettin was north of Berlin, and was a long drawn out mission with hours spent over enemy territory. We were not going over the North Sea, across Denmark then down to Stettin. The line on the map showed us going straight across Germany, right through the fighters and the flak. With that much time, probably about 8 hours, spent over enemy territory we were bound to run into fighters, and we were ready.

There was five gallons of jellied gasoline, buttressed with a quart of my Grandma's sorghum, in the toilet tank, and the lid tied down so it wouldn't flop off in evasive action. The bailing wire was rigged from the flush valve to the cockpit on the pilot's side. We even tied a red rag to the wire loop in the cockpit so the pilot could find it in a hurry. We were ready. It was a go.

Our Group put up 18 airplanes and the take-off and forming into Group formation was uneventful. We got into Wing formation and struck out across France in pretty tight formation. As the mission progressed and the pilots got tired the formation tended to scatter or open up, and our position, number 5 in the low squadron of the low group put us the lowest B-17 on the left side of the 56 ship Combat Wing. We were in an ideal position to test our theory, and the ammunition was ready and waiting.

Over Denmark we saw the first unfriendly fighters. They flew past us, circled ahead and made a half-hearted pass from head on. They disappeared behind us, probably to attack another wing, but five fighters continued to frail us looking for an opening to shoot somebody down. We had pulled our formation together, and they finally left us.

After dropping the bombs and turning north for our return we again became complacent. It was a beautiful sunny day, there was a lower overcast, and we were flying above the clouds, no fighters, and no flak. Everyone tended to relax if relaxing is possible in a combat situation 500 miles into enemy territory.

The unexpected happened, when two Me-109s came up through the clouds, and in a climbing position shot down two B-I7s in our group. Lt.Thomas R Francis in plane 42-97404 SU-L (544th Squadron) with 1 crewman killed in action, and nine prisoners of war. Lt. Charles W. Baker was the pilot in the second B-I7, 43-102548 with 3 killed in action and 7 prisoners.

The pilot, 2nd Lt. Thomas R. Francis probably went to his death, holding the burning airplane in a steady position so his crew could jump, and he stayed a few seconds longer than he should have. He probably wanted to make sure they were all out

In a few seconds 4 men are dead, some of the other crewmen wounded, and the prisoners in for almost a year of suffering in prison camps. The generals say that is a small price to pay for puffing the bombs on the target, but the names of Harry L. Gutierrez, Carroll D. Swartzendruber, and Salvatore Soto should be enshrined in stone and remembered forever. They were brave young men and they made the ultimate sacrifice.

The Me-I09s had darted up through the overcast fired into the bellies of the B-17s sending them spiraling down trailing smoke and fire. The German fighters had ducked right back into the under cast and disappeared. I told the crew to be alert, our plane being so low in the formation was a natural prey for the fighters. They would be anxious to add to their score, and we looked like easy pickings.

We opened our bomb bay doors, alerted the ball turret gunner to point his guns down and keep his eyes open. I let the copilot fly the airplane, and reached down and grabbed hold of the bailing wire that was threaded back to the toilet stool flush valve. The whole crew was tense, and apprehensive. In about a minute the ball turret gunner reported on the intercom, "Get ready, here comes one

My hand tightened on the bailing wire trigger, and regardless of the cold (minus 40 degrees Fahrenheit) I was sweating. The fighter

didn't have to be teased into position. He was climbing, coming at our belly, when the ball turret gunner yelled, "Now!"
I immediately jerked the bailing wire, and the ball turret gunner started firing. Out of the corner of my eye I saw a tremendous orange flash, and knew the jellied gasoline had been ignited. Looking down I saw the German fighter with all the fabric burned off the control surfaces, and the pilot wiggling the stick wondering what had happened to his control. The bombardier had a beautifiil view of the pilot, and he reported there was a puzzled look on his face. As the German fighter fell off on it's wing the pilot bailed out.
The crew was excited and happy, and they all started talking on the intercom at once. I warned them to be quiet, and not let down their guard; there were still German fighters in the area. We closed the bomb bay doors and moved back into formation.

Being low man in the formation it was obvious that no one else had seen our downing of the German fighter, and I didn't figure we could get a confirmation. As it turned out two other gunners in the formation in different planes claimed they had shot down a German fighter, and one of them got credit for it. The ball turret gunner told us that the jellied gasoline had come out perfectly, and he had been

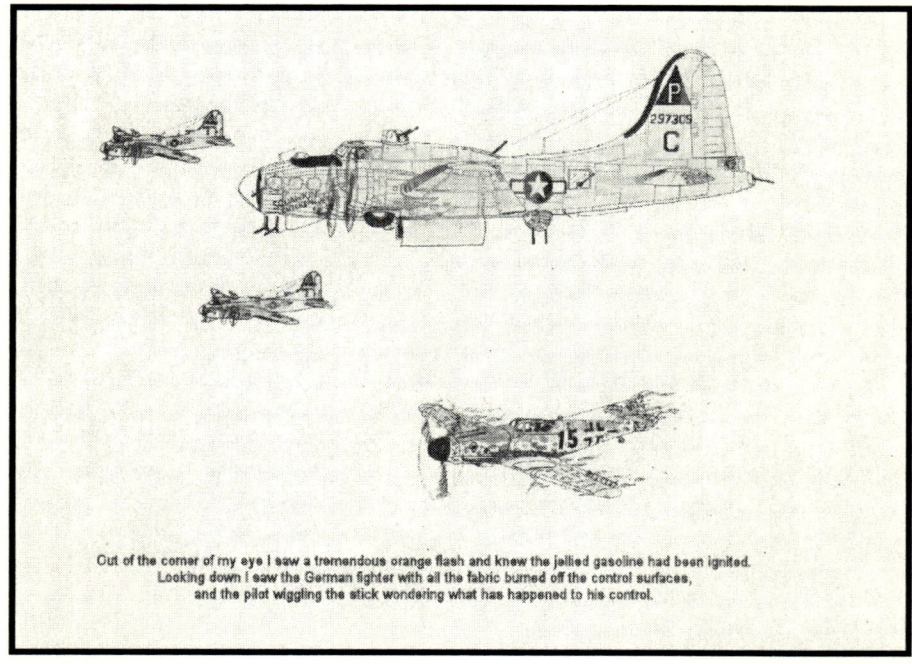

Out of the corner of my eye I saw a tremendous orange flash and knew the jellied gasoline had been ignited. Looking down I saw the German fighter with all the fabric burned off the control surfaces, and the pilot wiggling the stick wondering what has happened to his control.

quick to ignite it with his tracer fire. The explosion had caused him to lose sight of the German fighter temporarily, but he also had seen the plane with its scorched skin and the fabric burned off the control surfaces. He said the control surfaces were being rapidly moved in every direction as the pilot wiggled the stick, wondering what had happened.

Back at the base, we didn't talk much about it. The crew chief of the airplane was aware of what we were doing, and a few other enlisted men were privy to our secret. After we had gotten our third enemy fighter our crew chief painted three small toilets up under the pilots window. They were not prominent, but they could be seen from the ground. We were elated at our success, and were very proud of the fact that we burned off the control surfaces of the German fighters, and down they went with a puzzled pilot wiggling the stick around, wondering why he didn't have control of the airplane.

The West Pointers on the base were not aware of our success, and we thought they would probably frown at our method of delivering the lethal dose of jellied gasoline. However, the secret was getting harder and harder to contain. Most of the enlisted men on the base knew about our toilet, and thought it a pretty good joke.

In a couple of weeks we had our fifth enemy fighter down. We had five, which entitled us to call ourselves the Ace Crew, but the bloom was off the rose, and I was called to Headquarters to see the Commanding Officer. I expected a warm welcome, and congratulations, but instead I got my ass chewed out. He ordered me to take the toilet stool out of the bomb bay, and in no uncertain terms told me that I was a disgrace to the Army Air Corps Officers Corp. I was a disgrace to all the officers, who faithfully served, followed orders, used Government equipment that was issued to fight the Hun, and did not embarrass the Commanding Officer.

"That was my toilet your crew took. I've had to use the regular officers latrine." His face was red and his eyes were bulging. "What if the General heard about this, fighting the enemy with a toilet stool," he shouted.. "He probably would have my gawd damn eagles." I was crestfallen, but the crew and I quickly took out the toilet, took out the bailing wire trigger, and put the plane back in shape to fight the Hun in a more conventional manner. The tall old Colonel got his revenge. He must have been amused while he signed the order to give me the DEATH SENTENCE. He had given me an extra combat mission, (not the crew), and I flew 31 instead of 30 missions.

**Ben's Invention
"ACE MAKER – Glob Dropper"**

LUCKY

He was a coal black and mangy old dog. He had one eye (his left one I believe) out, one ear had been chewed off, he hopped around on three legs, and his tail had been broken. He had been castrated, and we called him "Lucky." He was aloof, kept to himself, but attached himself to the 545th Squadron. He had been around for sometime. A long time in combat years, and I have a picture of him I streaking past a parade honoring the transition of Grafton Underwood from the British to the United States Army Air Corps. This happened on July 4' 1943. In the picture you can see the black streak at the front of the formation, blurred and hard to see, but he's there.

Over the year, he had attached himself to various members of the 545th Squadron. Most of the crews he had watched over had survived, and the beat up mangy old black dog remained loyal to the 545th Squadron. He would sleep outside the barracks by day, and at night would wander from one plane to the next belonging to the 545th. He had grease all over him from being around the engine changes, but be would once in a while go into the crew chief's tent of a particular airplane and loaf while the crew worked on their plane. He knew which planes belonged to the 545th and that was where he spent his nights.

He would leave the flight line early in the morning, go to the mess hall (officers), and usually one of the cooks would give him a piece of steak or a ham sandwich. He then would go to the briefing room, and wait for the crews. He would pick a 545th crew, and would usually be at their hardstand by the time the truck arrived with the crew. When "Lucky" was at your hardstand it was considered a good omen. He would lay down near the crew chiefs tent and watch the preparations for the mission, and as soon as the planes were off the pound he would make his way to the 545th barracks where he would sleep outside the barracks while the mission was underway.

Invariably he would be on the hardstand he had picked that morning as the aircraft returned and made their pass over the field before landing. He would stand by the crew chiefs tent along with the mechanics, and intently watch the crew disembark. When all ten had left the plane, he showed no more interest and lay down. He didn't invite friendship, and avoided efforts of the crew to be friendly.

On April 13, 1944 the 545th Squadron was decimated. "Lucky" had visited our hardstand that morning, and we were the only crew to return out of seven planes that had been dispatched.. It was a blow to the entire 384 Bomb Group. Nine aircraft had gone down taking with them 90 crewmen and 28 of them had been killed in action. A few days later new crews started coming in as replacements. I'll never forget the reaction in "Lucky" when he saw Warren B May, navigator on the Jack Liebert crew. His one good ear raised a little, and the broken tail started wagging. That old messed up tail was going back and forth like a bandleader's baton on a fast dance tune "Lucky" had found someone to attach himself to, and he took to May like they had been friends forever.

May patted him on the head, and got grease on his hand. He had to be careful when he had pinks on and "Lucky" would get too close to him, and stain his pants. May and the ugly old black dog bonded and became almost inseparable. Where May went "Lucky" went. "Lucky" moved into our barracks and slept at the foot of May's bunk. At the mess hall May would load up on food and "Lucky" started gaining weight. It was funny seeing May walking down to the mess hall and old "Lucky" hopping along besides him. May was 19 years old, and old "Lucky," in dog years was probably old enough to be his grandfather. May talked to him all the time, and I swear you could detect a smile on the old dogs face.

Lucky only went to the hardstand when May was due to fly on a mission. When May got up and dressed on the cold damp English mornings "Lucky" would watch him intently, and then hop with him to the mess hall. "Lucky" would go with him to briefing, waiting outside, and then while May drew his flight gear the old dog would go right straight to the hardstand May would be flying from. Some of us knew this about the ugly old dog, that he had a sixth sense and could always find the right plane and hardstand. Tied up with our own fears and apprehensions we paid little attention to it.

On July 20th, 1944 the Liebert crew with Warren B. May as navigator took off for a mission to Nordhausen, Germany. Old "Lucky" watched the plane depart then laid down outside by the crew chiefs tent. He would lay there until the plane returned. On this day, however, at about 2 o'clock in the afternoon "Lucky" started moaning deep in his chest. He got to his feet and hopped and moaned in a circle around the hardstand, and the mechanics knew immediately that their plane had probably gone down. Finally the old dog sat down on his crooked leg, put his head back, and let out a plaintive howl and then started to the 545th barracks area. He was never seen again.

When the B-17s of the 384th returned the Liebert crew aircraft was among them. The plane was firing red flares, and was allowed to make an emergency landing, and the ambulance rushed to the hardstand to care for the wounded. There was no one wounded, but in the bloodstained nose at the navigator's station, Warren B. May was dead. His head nearly blown away.

Today, many years later, with nothing left of the field but a broken up runway and a few hardstands the people of the little village hear things. When the mists hang low, it's cold and damp outside they hear faint sounds of engines being run up, and the laughter of young men. They pull the covers over their heads however, when they hear the howling of an ugly old black dog that nobody has seen.

THE STORY OF ASCEND CHARLIE

The 14th mission, September 16th, 1943, did not get much publicity and no mention is made of the combat losses. The combat report is as follows:

"More than 130 heavy bombers attack port area and Chateau-Bougon airfield, more than 70 hit La Pallice harbor installations and Laleu airfield near La Rochelle, 21 strike at Cognac/Chateaubernard air field. Nearly 70 medium bombers attack Beaumont-le-Roger and Triqueville. Five B17s fly night mission with 340 RAF heavy bombers against Modane marshaling yard. This mission is flown from the United Kingdom at the request of General Eisenhower. Three B-24 Groups in the United Kingdom (44th, 93rd and 388th) are sent on loan to North Africa at General Eisenhower's request for support of the crucial campaign in this theater."

Major Gemmill and Lt. Geary were leading the 390th Bomb Group. They were flying in B-17 230434 and were responsible for maintaining 150 miles per hour, keeping their relative position in the 13th Combat Wing flying with the 95th and the 100th Bomb Groups. They were to maintain the altitude, and not speed up causing the group to spread out and straggle. At the target the groups split up each one bombing on its own, and the pilot was responsible for maintaining the 150 miles per hour airspeed, and the altitude, while the bombardier guided the plane with his Norden bomb sight. When the lead bombardier, in the lead plane, dropped his bombs the rest of the group triggered their bombs,

Lt. Geary was off the ground at 1112. He climbed out, making a slight turn so his squadron members could catch him. The squadrons assembled, joined the group, and the group then joined the Combat Wing. This is all done with split-second timing, and good navigation. 1st Lt. Gus Mencow was the lead navigator in Geary's plane.

The mission started on a sour note. Because of the weather the Combat Wing flew 25 miles to the left of the briefed course. This was a long mission. About 1,400 miles round trip, and the longest the 390th had flown at that time. Leaving England the Wing came back on course, but was soon to the left of course about 30 miles, and entered the enemy coast about 10 miles north of the briefed course. The target to be attacked was the aircraft factory on the airfield at Bordeaux, The secondary was the airfield at Cognac, and the last resort a factory on the northern outskirts of Bordeaux. The situation now changed as they approached the target. Enemy fighter planes were seen but only one made a pass at the formation. Bad luck took over, and clouds obscured all the targets. No bombs were dropped on the primary, secondary, or the last resort. It had been a futile exercise, and as the bombers turned away the bombs hung by their shackles in the bomb bays. Twenty-one aircraft went over the primary, secondary and the target of last resort, and they all failed to drop because of the weather. Rather than drop indiscriminately over France, the bombs were jettisoned on the way back. Two planes in the group did bomb targets of opportunity. Number 230330, flown by Lt. Wade H. Sneed, dropped on some flak barges off the coast of La Rochelle, and 23327, flown by Lt. Asmussen, dropped on a target of opportunity at La Pallice.

There were fighter planes in the area of Bordeaux, and heavy flak was encountered at the Ii de Re Island and La Pallice. It must have been in this area at about 1800 hours that 25903, **Ascend Charlie**, was hit.

Ascend Charlie was seen near La Rochelle with the number 1 engine feathered. There was much damage to the nose. She was last seen three minutes before the Group made landfall at the English coast. And here the mystery deepens. The 390th Bomb Group stayed on a northeast course, and **Ascend Charlie,** now having descended to about 1,000 feet turned almost straight north. She had no radio contact, one engine out, damage to the nose and pilot area of the plane. The weather was bad as Gus Mencow reported that: *"30 miles before Lizzard's Point, ran into a storm and lost formation."*

This meant that the other B-17s had to get to Parham and the 390th Bomb Group air field as best they could. Seven planes of the group landed at alternate bases.

Ascend Charlie, with one engine out, flying at about 1,000 feet hurtled through the overcast sky on a northerly heading. What went on aboard the plane is a question that will never be answered. Something must have happened to the navigator, 2nd Lt. Robert I Schanen, as he would never have turned to the heading they were flying. By dead reckoning he would have directed them on a heading that would have lead to the 390th airfield. The lack of radio communication with the other planes and the ground prevented them from getting a heading to their station. Ascend Charlie droned on into the overcast, headed for a sudden and tragic end. She was alone, carrying a dead and wounded crew, headed north, and the rest of the group flying north of London headed for East Anglia.

Let me quote from a letter written August 4, 1993 by Howell Davies to the author. Mr. Davies was a young man living in Gilwern near where **Ascend Charlie** crashed:

"On 16th September 1943 1 was enjoying a last smoke outside my home in Gilwern with a few buddies. It was 9:30 and we had just cycled back 'from the Air Cadet evening class at the local township of Crickhowell. It was dusk and the clouds were low with a light drizzle beginning to fall. From the South, very low, but hidden in the murk, a heavy sounding aircraft flew overhead. The sound died away in the distance, then we saw a dull orange glow from the high ground to the North. Seconds later came the sound of a muffled explosion. We knew that the aircraft had gone in. The next day we heard the worst. An American 'Flying Fortress' had crashed into one of the ridges of the 'Black Mountains' some six or seven miles to the North.

On a Saturday a friend and I cycled (our only personal transport in those days), through the lanes of the remote but beautiful 'Vale of

Grwyney' up to and beyond the hamlet of Llanbedr. As we approached the closed in 'dead end' of the valley we could see high on the ridge the tail section of the aircraft, the fin still pointing up to the sky."

1st Lt. Herbert I. Turner was the pilot of 42-5903, Ascend Charlie. He was a native of Florida, and finished high school in Ocala. He then went to Marysville (Tenn.) College, and was accepted as an aviation cadet in 1940. His childhood friend Fred Turner went into the Air Corps with Herbert and served in the Pacific. Herbert's first flying training began at Sumter, S. C., and then to Murfreesboro, Tenn. He finished advanced at Turner Field in Albany, Ga. December 12, 1942, and proudly pinned on the 2nd Lt.'s bars. On December 13, 1942 at the First Methodist Church in Albany, he married a beautiful young lady who became Lee Turner. She followed him to Epharta then Spokane, Washington, and finally to Salina, Kansas, where Herbert was assigned overseas. Lee Turner was 6 months pregnant when 'Ascend Charlie' slammed into the Black Mountains in Wales. She later gave birth to a son Herbert Turner Ill. Herbert Turner III served honorably in the Vietnam War.

Fred Turner returned from the war, having served, with the 20th Air Force, and married Lee Turner. He adopted Herbert Turner 111, and they had two lovely daughters.

Mrs. Turner has a letter from 1st Lt E. W. Weldon, Jr., a member of the 390th, written a few days after the accident:

"Ascend Charlie had the number three spot in the lead element, and I was right over him in the second. Our squadron was high in the group. No opposition was encountered until we reached the target. I was busy there and it wasn't until we turned for home that I saw Lefty's (Turner's) number two engine smoking.

He waited a long time before feathering it. A ship with a propeller stopped is an invitation to fighters and he didn't want to bring us any more trouble. On three engines he had to slow down, but the whole squadron dropped back and wouldn't let him leave the formation. On the long trip home everything appeared to be well in hand. There were injured men aboard but Lefty flew beautiful formation and kept giving us the old hi sign.

Night enveloped us before landfall and we had to disperse the formation on account of bad weather. With his ship crippled, gas low and Schanen (the navigator) wounded Lefty never made it home."

2nd Lt. Frederick M. Broers was the copilot on Ascend Charlie. Lt. Robert L Schanen was the navigator from Port Washington, Wisconsin. He was an exceptional young man, having attended the University of Wisconsin where he had earned a Bachelor of Law degree in 1941. He was licensed to practice law before all courts in Wisconsin, including the Supreme Court, and federal courts of the state. He loved his profession, but gave it up to fight and die for his country.

1st Lt Turner, pilot; and 2nd Lt. Boers had each flown 8 of the 390th Bomb Group's 13 missions. The Bordeaux mission had been number 14. 1st Lt. Orval Tofte, the bombardier, 8 missions.; S/Sgt Phillip Catania, radio operator, 8 missions.; S/Sgt. Sherman E. Rambo, top turret gunner, 8 missions; S/Sgt. Stanley B. Mason, left waist gunner, 7 missions with this crew; S/Sgt. John 1. Peterson, 8 missions with this crew; and S/Sgt. Alfred C. Monson, tail gunner, 8 missions with this crew.

In a strange coincidence, and what happened many times in a combat group, S/Sgt. Robert B. Oremus, ball turret gunner, from Rochester, N.Y, was an original crew member and had flown 8 missions with the crew of **Ascend Charlie.** He had flown every mission they flew from the start of operations, but on the mission to Bordeaux (the 14th mission for the Group) he was not assigned to this crew, and was replaced by Sgt. Swen A. Zertterberg, ball turret gunner, from Rockford, Ill. This was his 7th mission having flown with crew 46 three times, 41 once, 44 twice, and finally the fatal last mission with crew 41. The strange hand of fate that allowed S/Sgt. Oremus to live, and Sgt. Swen A Zetterberg to die happened many times with crews of the mighty Eighth Air Force in Europe. Someone got sick, he was replaced and the plane went down killing the entire crew.

Cecil S. Holliday's feelings about the loss of **Ascend Charlie**'s crew is best revealed in a letter he wrote to Mr. Davies September 4, 1993:

"...I remember well the day Turner's crew went in. I can not remember the details of the mission or even if our crew flew that day, but I remember the loss we felt that night with the empty bunks caused by their absence. The war and flying was all a game up to that time, from that time we felt the loss and stress of flying combat. In such circumstances, the loss of a close friend in combat, it caused you to wonder if there had been something you had done to contribute to their loss. If there might have been something you could have done to avert the disaster. All of these things run around in your mind as you set and look at the empty bunks. I don't remember if our crew chatted among themselves, but if we did I am sure it was in their honor.

When the Squadron Commander's crew came to clean out their personal belongings they ran us out of the Q-Huts. I remember how I resented their actions; they had no right to their personal stuff. We resented the strangers doing something we felt we should have done. We would have packed their things with care and tender love as if we were dealing with them personally, not just put it in a box with indiscretion. This, of course was done, but we felt it was not."

A total of about 58 men were killed in action September 16, 1943 including Turner's crew. Their possessions were packed up and shipped home, and the telegrams were sent to the grieving families. A form letter was sent home with the commanding officer's signature, bodies were brought home at the end of the war, and their names were slowly forgotten.

Over the years George Pemberton and Howell Davies had been intrigued by the story of **Ascend Charlie** and they had made attempts to find crew member's next of kin. As the years passed they planned a 50th anniversary dedication in honor of the 10 men. A plaque would be mounted on the wall in the Church of Llanbedr, listing all their names with suitable wording. The little Church at Llanbedr had stood for centuries and was at the foot of, the ridge where **Ascend Charlie** crashed. It is almost certain the church will be there many more years, and the names of this crew will not soon be forgotten.

The plaque was designed and manufactured information was sent out about the dedication to be held Sept. 16th 1993. It was thought that an American Air Force representative would be appropriate to unveil the memorial. Mr. Davies had written to the chief of public relations at USAF Mildenhall. They referred the request to Upper Hayford, the nearest Air Force base. The rector even contacted the US Embassy in London, but all to no avail. An attempt was made by the 390th Memorial Museum to get the chaplain of the 77th Fighter Group, then stationed in England, to attend, but never heard from them.

Let me now quote from a letter Howell Daves wrote to George Jahnke, a 390th Bomb Group member:

Firstly a few words about the service. Both Gorden Pembridge and myself were pleasantly surprised when about a hundred people turned up at the church. Llanbedr is a very small village, off the beaten track, in one of the beautiful but remote (for Britain) valleys, in the Black Mountain range, which in these parts form the natural border between South Wales and England (County of Herefordshire on the English side).

Everything went as planned. The singing was strong and good. The Rector of Llanbedr, Rev. Christopher Blanchard, who incidentally had fully supported Gordon and myself in our project to see a plaque erected, carried out his part with feeling and dignity. His wife Tanya read one of Bob Schanen's poems. A young lady air cadet, Helen Trick, from the Abergavenny, (local town), Squadron of the A. T. C. (Air Training Corps), unveiled the plaque and the Rector offered a prayer of dedication commemoration, reading out the names of Lt. Turner and his crew, virtually fifty years almost to the minute, that the young men had perished on the nearby mountain range.

No American representative was present when the service started. However, after a few minutes of the commencing of the service a tall leather jacketed young man with a military bearing entered the church. His name was Capt. Phil Kovach and he was a helicopter pilot in the United States Marine Corps, presently on an exchange posting with the Royal Navy.

Howell Davis in a letter to Capt. Kovach September 26, 1993 explains about their unsuccessful efforts to enlist an American representative and then says:
"Then, on the night and out of no-where, so to speak, you arrived. Believe me, there were those present who saw the hand of God in your presence."

We searched for and found Major Phil Kovach who is still a proud pilot for the US Marine Corps. He told us that he had just landed from a training sortie that afternoon, and went directly to the church in his flight gear: *"complete with naval leather flight jacket, sun glasses and 'piss cutter garrison cover (hat). I was just there as a curious 'Yank' to be a fly-on-the-wall and to see what it was all about. I became the focus of the whole event (not withstanding the immortal crew of **Ascend Charlie**.) Those folks looked like they had seen a ghost when I came sauntering into town... I was very moved by the fateful flight of **Ascend Charlie** and her crew, and especially touched and honored as an American that these good people of Wales took it upon themselves to memorialize these heroes of our sometimes neglectful country."*

THE BAILEY CREW

What thoughts went through the mind of 1st Lt. Everett L. Bailey in the early morning hours of April 24, 1944 are unknown. Certainly he was tense, and apprehensive about the mission. He was concerned about the aircraft he was to fly; his position in the formation, and especially, he was concerned about the new crew he had been assigned to fly with him. None of the crew had been in combat except the Navigator, Lt. Charles D. Wallach, who had four missions.

Bailey's first chance to talk to the crew was at the aircraft they were scheduled to fly. He assembled them under the wing and explained to them what he expected. Keep alert, stay off the intercom, unless an airplane gets to close in the formation, or if you see fighter planes. He instructed them to call out all fighter planes even our own "Little Friends, and no screaming or shouting over the intercom in the excitement of a fighter attack. He did his best to prepare them for the possible fear and horror of the coming combat mission. He was experienced and 4 missions away from finishing his tour of duty. Whatever emotions he felt, while talking to the crew, he kept to himself. He was composed and calm while instructing them on procedures and conduct he wanted.

He was flying "Little Chubb," 42-102446 JD-M from the 545th Squadron. He was flying number 2 in the lead squadron of the high group in the 41st "B" Combat Wing. Laboda was flying number 3, Deputy Group Lead, and could take over if Capt. Langlois, Group Leader, was shot down. Lt. Bailey was probably put in the number 2 spot because of his inexperienced crew.

Take off and assembly was routine and soon the bomber stream was lined out for miles headed for the target at Oberpfaffenhofen. It was an awesome sight to see the sun glinting on the wings of the hundreds of Fortresses all in a row except for the 41st "B" flying all by itself to the right of 41 "A".

Lt. Bailey struggled along with the inevitable fighter attack near Stuttgart left him with one engine out, the nose damaged, and a wounded Bombardier. He attempted to keep up with the formation, but slowly dropped back further and further. He elected to go to Switzerland.

There was much fighter activity in the area, and a lone B-17 was an inviting target. A few minutes before he was surrounded by his friends. Looking in any direction there had been big spinning props, and big planes bristling with 50 caliber machine guns. Now the sky was empty, and he felt exposed, naked, and vulnerable. He had a badly damaged plane, all alone in enemy territory, and had to maintain some altitude to get over the Alps. It was freezing cold but vapor drifted off his gloved hand holding the throttles. Lt. Bailey was sweating in spite of the cold.

Switzerland was a neutral country. If you flew into her territory, and landed the crew was interned for the duration of the war, and the aircraft was confiscated. The Swiss provided food, clothing, housing, and health care, and generally treated our personnel well. It was a safe haven for American heavy airplanes, wounded on board, with no option other than a prison camp, or death at the hands of German civilians.

When he finally got into Swiss airspace, Lt Bailey breathed a sigh of relief, and started looking for a place to land. He was letting down when six Swiss fighters appeared in the sky, and started circling "Little Chubb" like buzzards circling their prey.

Ll. Bailey was having trouble with one landing gear not extending. There were heavy gas fumes in the bomb bay from leaks in the wing tanks. One crew member reported that the rudder was jammed and Lt. Bailey could only turn to the right. The ball turret guns were straight down indicating that no one was in the ball turret. It's unlikely that any gunners were in their position, because they felt they were in safe territory.

Lt Bailey had circled The Greifensee, a lake southeast of Duhendorf. There was an airfield located at Dubendorf, used by the Swiss for heavy bombers. It was apparent that Lt. Bailey intended ditching in the lake rather than attempt a landing on one wheel. He circled the lake a second time, and the Swiss fighters moved in. As Lt. Bailey started a third pass, three of the fighters opened fire.

"Little Chubb' was doomed. She was at about 1000' and burning. Lt. Bailey immediately gave the bail out order. Eye witnesses said that all four engines were silent when the plane went over their heads, but the plane was burning badly. Lt. Bailey, Sgt Hollingsworth, and Sgt. Melazzi bailed out near The Greifensee. Lt. Bailey's body was found on the shore of the lake. His chute had failed to open. Sgt. Meiazzi died, but Sgt. Hollingsworth survived, his chute just opening in time. Sgt. Hollingsworth landed in a small village near the lake. S. Sgt. Newell and S. Sgt. Silag both parachuted out at low altitude, and although burned, and shaken up, both survived.

Lt Wallach was laying in the radio room. He had been badly wounded in the original German fighter attack, and again by the Swiss fighters. When "Littlie Chubb" hit the water, Lt. Wallach was thrown about 50 feet from the crash. He was rescued by two soldiers working nearby. Later he recovered, and escaped from Switzerland returning to the United States in November of 1944.

Lt. Burry was in the co-pilots seat, and Sgt. Pratt and Lt. Greenbaurn were standing between the pilot and co-pilots seats. LI. Greenbaurn had been wounded on the original German Fighter attack. It is believed that he, Pratt and Burry were killed by the Swiss fighters, and that Sgt Pratt and LI Greenbaum were ejected from the plane at the time of the crash.

The commander of the Swiss Air Force made several lame excuses for shooting down the American bomber obviously in trouble and attempting to land. He claimed that "Little Chubb" had tried to escape, and could have crashed into the city of Zurich. He also stated that American Bombers, three weeks before, had bombed the Swiss town of Schaffhausen on the border with Germany. Public opinion favored the American bomber crew.

It was a senseless, unnecessary attack, Americans paid the ultimate price for their fellowmen and their country.

In 1953 the pitiful remains of "Little Chubb" was raised from the bottom of the cold lake. She was 130 feet down. In the copilots seat were the remains of 2nd Ll. James Burry. He was given a heroes burial in a cemetery near Zurich on September 20, 1953.

It all happened--one April afternoon.

P	Everett L. Bailey	1st Lt.	KIA
CP	James E. Burry	2nd Lt.	KIA
N	Charles D. Wallach	2nd Lt.	RTD
B	Jesse L. Greenbaum	2nd Ll.	KIA
R.	William J. Silag	S/Sgt.	RTD
TT	Raymond A Newell	S/Sgt.	RTD
BT	Anthony T. Melazzi, Jr.	Sgt.	KIA
TG	Sidney J. Pratt	Sgt.	KIA
FG	Richard R. Hollingsworth	Sgt.	RTD
FG	Richard M. Sendlback	Sgt	KIA

LEGEND OF

HEWITT "BUCK" DUNN

He was born in Newport News, Virginia in 1921 and was a star athlete at Bethany College. He enlisted in the US Army Air Corp, became a gunner, and was ultimately assigned to the 390th Bomb Group. He started flying combat missions January, 29, 1944. He did not take a leave, time off, or return to the United States until the end of the war. He flew the astonishing total of 104 Combat Missions. According to an article in "Stars and Stripes" around early November, 1944 Buck Dunn had said, "I want to go home just as much if not more than any fellow, but I can't until the fight here is finished." He flew 104 combat missions in the European Theater for the 390th Bomb Group then when the war broke out in Korea he flew 64 more. There is little known about him outside of the 390th Group.

Consider other heroes:
Lt. Col. Immanuel Klette, of the 306th and 91st Bomb Groups, died Feb. 12, 1988. Because of his heroic war record of flying 91 missions with the 8th Air Force in WW II, he was buried in Arlington National Cemetery. His burial was given much publicity. The record says, "He flew more missions than any other pilot in the 8th Air Force."

Maurice "Mike" Malone from Spiro, Oklahoma, flew 29 missions with the 390th Bomb Group, 57lst Squadron. He started flying combat however, in Africa, and Italy. He flew 50 missions in his tour there. After returning to the United States he became a gunnery instructor training gunners combat tactics. He became bored doing this and volunteered for a tour in the 8th Air Force, and was assigned to the 390th Bomb Group to the Peter E. Stene's crew. This became a lead crew, and flying a PFF mission exploded over the channel on returning from the target. The entire crew was KIA except for Lt. Jim Keelan who parachuted into the water and was lucky enough to be picked up. "Mike" Malone had flown about 15 missions with this crew, and was upset that all his friends had died. In all, he flew 29 missions with the 390th making a total of 79 missions to his credit.

Master Sgt. Clarence Campbell, of the 401st Bomb Group, had a difficult time getting into the service. He had a bad back, had several children, and was 30 years old. He tried the Army, Navy, Marines, and finally on his 14th try he succeeded in enlisting in the US Army Air Corp. Like "Buck" Dunn he wanted combat. He flew 50 missions in Italy, and then transferred to the 8th Air Force. If headquarters stood him down to long, he would complain to the commanding officer who would see he got on a mission. On a leave he went with his brother, who was an infantry officer, He spent two weeks with the advancing US infantry in France. He flew a total of 32 missions with the 401st making his total 82 combat missions.

"Buck" Dunn:
There is a story, told by Col. Moller, when he (Col. Moller) encountered "Buck" Dunn near the "Rocker Club" (the NCO club) late one evening. Dunn had an enlisted man, passed out, under each arm. He dropped the two men, and executed a proper salute to the Col. without missing a beat he picked up the two enlisted men and continued on his way.

Several years ago, at a Tucson Reunion, a bombardier (I have forgotten his name) told me about the briefing for bombardiers. They would watch "Buck" Dunn. He would come into the briefing room, set down in a chair and lean back, using the back two legs of the chair. After the curtain was drawn and the target was exposed if Dunn stayed leaned against the wall, the other bombardiers relaxed. It was a milk run. However if Dunn leaned forward and had all four legs of the chair on the floor, then the bombardiers knew it was a tough mission. Their apprehensive levels went sky high, and they sweated out the mission.

In the 390th Veterans Association/Foundation Newsletter for the summer of 1990, William M. MacVicar, co-pilot, 569th Squadron wrote an article "Not So Typical Day in The Life of A Bomber Crew." He writes about "Buck" Dunn, flying on his 94th mission (3-21-45) as top turret/engineer, for his first and only time in that position, becoming unhooked from his oxygen regulator and collapsing in the top turret. Because of his size he had fallen with his head in a position difficult to get an oxygen mask on. The pilot, Lt. Mel Meyers, got out of his seat to administer oxygen to "Buck" now passed out himself. The co-pilot (MacVicar) was diving the plane to get to a lower altitude, and the navigator helped revive the two downed crewman. They had left the formation, and headed for home. Lt. Meyers revived, and flew the plane home. He ultimately received a Distinguished Flying Cross for helping out a downed crewman.

Dick Cowles flew about 15 missions with "Buck" Dunn, and had a great admiration for him. Dick Cowles maintains that "Buck" could anticipate and call out flak bursts, and tells the story of a mission to Duisburg, Germany, 1-28-45. Just before the target a four gun battery had fired, and "Buck" Dunn had called out, "Watch out they are going to get us!" The bursts ahead of them were bigger than 88mm, and were probably 155mm. The next bursts (about 20 seconds later) one shell went through the floor and the ceiling of the radio room. It exploded just above the plane. The next four gun burst was behind Dick Cowle's tail gunner's position. Lt. Shira, the pilot, called all positions on the intercom to access the damage. The plane had shot up in altitude when the shell exploded, and slammed down just as suddenly. Only Dick Cowles answered the pilots call on the interphone. The pilot told him to come forward and check out the damage. Cowles crawled out of his position with a walk around bottle, and found both waist gunners out. He administered to them and then went forward to the radio room. There was tangled metal around the ball turret, one side of the radio room bulkhead was blown out, and the radio transmitters were gone. The radio man was on the floor. Cowles remembers seeing a tangled mess of control cables the radio room bulkhead gone, and tangled metal over the ball turret. Cowles first got oxygen to the radio man, then called the pilot and notified him of the damage. Lt. Shira had put the plane on automatic pilot, and came to the back to access the damage to the control cables. He wanted to ascertain what the two remaining intact cables controlled, the elevators, the rudder, or the trim tabs. Then with help from a revived crewmember they removed the ball turret gunner who was OK. Without hesitation Lt. Shira continued over the target, flying on automatic pilot, and "Buck" Dunn triggered the bombs away when the group dropped. This was Dunn's 83rd mission, and none of them had been easy.

Hewitt "Buck" Dunn deserves the honored place in the 390th Memorial Museum. He is the only one that our Museum forefathers have authorized a special plaque for. He is an honest to God hero, and did what no other of the 300,000 members of the Mighty 8th Air Force did. He stands head and shoulders above the rest. There were 42 bomb groups in the 8th Air Force. There was one man who managed to fly 104 combat missions.

"Buck" Dunn has been shoved aside in history. We have told you he liked alcohol, and it contributed to his tragic death in Merced County, California , CA (Castle Air Base) in 1961. He was 40 years old. I would like to know where he is buried, and if his record is engraved on the tombstone.

There is no one else in the 8th Air Force with that kind of record. To survive 25, 30, or 35 missions in the 8th Air Force, meant much sweating (despite 50 degrees below zero temperatures), no sleep, and apprehensive morning activities before the missions. To some it was like a death sentence. To some it was a death sentence. "Buck" Dunn did it 104 times flying first initially as a tail gunner (32 missions), a waist gunner (one mission), as top turret (one mission) and a toggelier (70 missions). He was one of a kind.

THE SHORT LIFE OF WILLIAM W. SEITZ

I don't know when Bill Seitz was born or where he was from, but I know exactly where and when he died. He was probably close to my age when we were in the Aviation Cadet Program probably about 21 or 22 years of age. Our paths paralleled for about 36 weeks from mid 1943 to early 1944. We took basic training at Marana AAFB together, then to advanced training at Douglas AAFB, where on August 19, 1943 we were commissioned 2nd Lieutenants in the United States Army Air Corp. Both of us went to Roswell AAFB, New Mexico for B-17 transition training. We learned how to fly the "Queen of the Sky," the beautiful B-17, and then to Salt Lake City, Utah to pick up the nine handsome, very young, members of our crew. Our crew and combat formation flying training was conducted at Dalhart AAFB, Dalhart Texas. We flew countless hours of formation (in lightly loaded airplanes), cross country navigation training, and false bomb runs on Denver, Colorado, Los Angeles, and Dallas, Texas. After all that Bill Seitz and me were pretty friendly.

We went to Kearny, Nebraska, picked up brand new airplanes, and headed overseas, I never saw Bill Seitz again. After reaching England Bill was assigned to the 92nd Bombardment Group at Podington. I was assigned to the 384th Bombardment Group at Grafton Underwood. We both arrived at our respective bases in March of 1944, and both of us were flying combat in April of 1944.

The 92nd was one of the early groups in the European Theatre of Operations going overseas (flying their own planes) and were assigned to Bovington where they stayed until May 11, 1943. Then to Alconbury until September of 1943. They ended the war at Podington, and closed this base July 9, 1945. Because of their early entry into combat the 92ndwas assigned to train new groups m combat flying, and the 95th Bombardment Group was assigned to Alconbury in May 1943 for training from the 92nd

The dangers involved in getting a group of B-17s ready for combat were many. We were dealing with 2800 gallons of high octane aviation fuel in each plane, 7,000 rounds of 50 caliber ammunition, usually ten 500 pound bombs in the bomb bay, and fifteen 425 PSI pure oxygen bottles. It was a lethal, highly explosive mixture, waiting for the one mistake. New pilots, not accustomed to the heavily loaded airplanes, suffered mightily from apprehension (fear) and nervousness until they had taken the lethal heavily loaded B-17 down the runway for take off. Until you got your speed up the airplane was sluggish, and it was constantly on the mind of the pilot that one mistake meant the doom of 10 young men Imagine, if you will, that you are at the controls of a flying gasoline tanker, loaded with high explosives, and you are going to exceed 100 MPH on the runway. The runway was going to look short and the end came up real fast. It was nerve wracking when fog hung over the length of the runway, and you had to climb 2 or 3,000 feet to break out at the top of the overcast. The mission was only starting the scary stuff came later

On May 27, 1943 the 95th Bombardment Group suffered a horrible catastrophe, one of the worst of the war, while in training at Alconbury. The ground crews were loading the planes for the next days mission. It would have been their first with the 92nd Bombardment Group. The engines were being run up, fueling was underway, radios being checked, and ordinance being loaded. The ground crew was going about their duties enthusiastically doing work that they had spent many hours practicing. They were shouting back and forth, but no horseplay, as they realized the seriousness of the work they were doing.

Suddenly, without warning, ship number 2-29685 exploded with a horrifying sickening blast. Plane number 2-29685 just disappeared taking her ground crew with her Debris rained from the sky, and shock waves radiated out from the center of the blast destroying and killing in it's wake. Nineteen men died, and twenty were seriously injured. The devastating blast had killed at random with no rhyme or reason. An ordinance officer was found some distance away. There was not a mark on him he was killed by the concussion. An engineer, standing with a group of men, fell to the ground dead while the others lived. One combat crew, laying on the ground near their plane were not touched, but the navigator, Lt Frank Metzger, had been setting up and was dead from the concussion. This crew's plane was broken in two and completely separated. Four other B-17s were completely destroyed, and eleven others were wrecked beyond repair. The engines of 2-29685 were never found, and some of the other engines were driven deep into the ground. Here in one second went the lives of nineteen highly trained ground crewmen; that would be hard to replace.

The cause has never been determined. Many men who were there at the time have passed on and the names of the dead are slowly being forgotten, which is a pity. The 95th Bombardment Group went on to fly 321 combat missions with good and bad fortune in the air. They had a distinguished combat record.

The 92nd Bombardment Group moved to Podington, and my friend William W. Seitz was assigned there sometime in March of 1944. He had started his combat missions in April of 1944.

In early May of 1944 a chain of events occurred that directly effected and ended the life of Bill Sietz. On a mission to Berlin, May 8,1944 a young 92nd Bomb Group pilot, Jack Pearl, had turned back before the target and returned to the 92nd Bomb Group minus his co pilot, bombardier, and navigator. Lt Pearl reported that, "All four of his superchargers had run away." He had broken formation and turned back. At the Belgium coast they had encountered severe flak 2nd Lt. Robert J. Marcus, co pilot; Lt. Carl Palumbo, bombardier; and F/O Fred C Grant, navigator had bailed out over the cold, deadly water of the English Channel. Lt. Pearl could give no explanation or reason for the bail outs. He had not ordered the bail out. He was so busy flying the plane that he had not known they had bailed out. With the help of the crew he landed the plane with one engine out and another cutting in and out.

The mystery of why the three officers bailed out was never solved. To add to the mystery only two parachutes were used.

On May 19, 1944 the 92nd was again scheduled to go to Berlin. A young pilot, Lt. Pearl, was heard to say, "I've put in four missions since I joined the Group and every one has been to Berlin. So tomorrow sure as hell, it will be a "milk run" and I won't be on it."

The next day, May 20, 1944, was a "milk run" scheduled for Orly airfield, south of Paris. Due to last minute changes Lt. Pearl was selected. His wish to go on a "milk run" was granted. It cost him his life and set in motion the second great tragedy almost to a year for the 92nd Bomb Group.

It started out as a cold misty English morning. There was an overcast with a low ceiling of about 300 feet, and the tops at about 800 feet. Our crew was not on the mission, but were flying a weather ship reporting the overcast ceiling and tops. The ground had patchy fog on the runway, and visibility was not that good. It was early in the morning, very little wind, but a trailer had been stationed at the end of the runway to give the pilots a green light before take off

Several 92nd B-17s had gotten into the air, and it looked like a routine Group take off situation, but then came the turn of Lt. Pearl. He roared down the runway with a full load of gas, bombs and ammunition. It is unclear if he ever got off the runway, but he crashed into trees and a small village past the end of the runway. His gasoline exploded, and the plane was an inferno, but his bombs had not exploded. The next B-17 in line was my friend Bill Seitz, and since we took off in 30 second intervals, Bill was moving before Lt. Pearl crashed.

The take off controller on the field started firing red flares, and the control tower told him to stop his take of and he was able to stop about half way down the runway. He turned his plane around to taxi back to a turn off, and was looking death in the face. His last sight was a fully loaded B- 17 coming straight toward him. Hugh propellers chewing off the nose, and coming toward him. Then death.

1st Lt. James E. Wiggins did not stop his take off run. He missed the flares and didn't hear the calls from the tower. He had gotten the green light from the trailer and from his training had automatically reacted. When he saw Lt. Seitz's fortress it was too late. The two airplanes collided head on and burst into flames.

There were 10 men on each crew. Five crew members escaped from each plane. They were in the rear of the planes. Three minutes after the crash there were five terrific explosions. Each B-17 carried six 1000 pound bombs. Lt Seitz's and Lt. Wiggin's bombs exploded first, the last to explode were Lt Pearl's which was the first to crash.

I unknowingly lost my close personal friend, William Seitz, in the big black cloud above the field as I was flying above. It took three days to repair the landing field even in an expedited effort.

THE SETTLES FAMILY STORY

It was 8:30 PM on a quiet Sunday evening in Copeland, Kansas. The date was September 17, 1944. In the Copeland Methodist Church the Reverend Marshall R. Hinds was preaching to his congregation.

"Every valley shall be exalted, and every mountain and hill shall be made low; the crooked shall be made straight, and the rough places plain." As he talked the Reverend's voice became inaudible, overwhelmed by the horrible earth shaking roar of a giant four engine bomber flying at tree top level over the little village of Copeland. In seconds the bomber, about one-half mile from town, started a shallow turn to the right. A wing tip or propeller hit the ground, and the plane started burning.

Orice Dean Settles was born January 25, 1919 and died August 20, 1990. He was born and raised in Kansas, and married a beautiful young farm girl, Ruth Hatfield, just before he went into the US Army Air Crop in 1942. After receiving his commission and wings in early 1943 he attended B-17 transition school. He had been trained to fly the B-17 "Flying Fortress; was assigned a crew, and went to combat training school. Here he would fly formation with other B-17s, the gunners would sharpen their gunnery skills, and the bombardier would simulate bombing US cities. They would fly long cross-country missions for navigation training, and generally get acquainted with the machine that would take them into combat.

In November of 1943 they went overseas, and were assigned to the Eighth Air Force, Third Division, 13th Combat Wing, 390th Bombardment Group, 570th Squadron. They were assigned living quarters, issued equipment, indoctrinated into group policy, lectured by experienced combat crewmen who had finished their tour of duty, and required to fly practice missions. All this was necessary before they would fly their first mission.

Orice Dean Settles had a distinguished and honorable combat record. He flew 30 combat missions and on eight of them was the Group Lead Pilot. A Group Lead pilot had 18 to 20 four engine heavy bombers behind him. He usually flew in the high or low group (18 to 20 airplanes) in a Combat Wing of 56 to 60 four engine B-17s. It required great skill to hold the airplane at exactly 150 miles per hour (true air speed) and his altitude at exactly 21,000 feet or whatever the assigned altitude was. He had to do this in order to hold his group in a tight formation. In addition he was required to hold his position in the Combat Wing. He had to keep his 18 airplanes in position on the Combat Wing leader at all times. If he got his speed up to 160 MPH there was great danger of scattering his formation, and leaving those in the rear end straggling and struggling to move back into formation. Under the most viscous fighter attacks, the leader sat straight and level, concentrating on holding the Group in tight formation. It was a stressful job. Settles did it eight times in some very rough missions:

Date	A/C	Target	Air Commander
2-4-44	239927	Frankfurt,Gr.	Col. Jeffery
3-9-44	231728	Berlin,Gr.	Maj. Gemmil
4-1-44	231728	Ludwigshafen,Gr.	Maj. S. O. Jones
4-22-44	231728	Hamm,Gr.	Maj. Gemmil
4-27-44	2102533	LeCulot,Fr.	Maj. W. Jones
5-1-44	2102533	Sarregumines,Fr.	Col. Ott
5-9-44	231728	LeonAthies,Fr.	Col. Ott
5-28-44	2102634	Magdeburg,Gr.	Col. Ott

His 30 combat missions were rough. They were filled with experienced enemy fighter pilot action, and extended bomb runs through bone chilling cold, and flak riddled skies over enemy targets. In his 30 combat missions enemy fighters and flak blasted 29 390th B-17s out of the sky. In the same 30 missions 390th gunners brought down 68 enemy fighter planes. The two missions that stood out for savage attacks by fighters were his 2nd to Emden on December 5th 1943, and his 29th to Magdeburg on May 28, 1944. On those two days the 390th lost 5 bombers and shot down 10 enemy fighters and 5 bombers and shot down 11 enemy fighters respectively.

On June 6, 1944 ("D" Day) he flew his last combat mission, and soon headed home to his wife and baby son. He was a happy man looking forward to time with family, a 30 day leave, and 10 days at an an Army Air Corp resort hotel in Santa Monica, California. He then would return to the 390'" Bombardment Group having signed up for another tour of duty. He returned to Copeland, Kansas where his wife, Ruth, and his baby son (soon to be one year old) were living with her dad and mother. Hen father owned a large farm, and it was located one-half mile south of Copeland, Kansas.

The big B-29 that roared, so low, across Copeland, Kansas that Sunday night on September 17, 1944 was stationed at Walker Army Air Field, Kansas. The tail number was 26379, meaning it
Was built in 1942, and was the $6,379^{th}$ plane built that year. It belonged to the 2nd Air Force, 500th (VH) Bombardment Group, 883rd Bombardment Squadron. The crew consisted of the following:

Pilot	Cooper, Wayne B.	2/Lt.
CoPilot	Eslinger, Lawrence H.	2/Lt.
Flight Engineer	Kane, William P.	2/Lt.
Nav./Bomb.	West, Kenneth 0	2/Lt.
Radio Operator	Gutt, Bruno (NM1)	Sgt.
Radar Operator	Johnson, George V.	Sgt.
Gunner	Cooper, Robert L.	Cpl.
Side Gunner	Kelly, John F.	Cpl.
Tail Gunner	Murphy, Gerald J.	Cpl.
Rear Gunner	Boston, Clarence A.	Cpl.

B-29, 26379 had taken off from US. Army Air Field, Walker, Kansas at 1754 CWT (5:54 PM) with 5,470 gallons of fuel and weighing 120,686 pounds. Their flight plan cleared them for an air to ground gunnery mission followed by a formation flight with another B-29. The bombardier, Lt. H. R. Weben, on 26379 had become ill in flight, and the plane had landed at 1926 CWT (7:26 PM) at Walker. The ill bombardier, Lt. Weber, was removed and the plane took off again at 1941 CWT (7:4 1 PM). Unfortunately the B-29 they were to fly practice formation with was unable to take off. B-29, 26379 was instructed to fly local instrument practice.

Those instructions meant flying in the local flying area, but Walker Army Air Force Base did not have a radio range station. It was accepted practice to go beyond the local flying area to utilize the radio range facilities of neighboring stations for simulated instrument practice. There were a number of these stations within 100 miles. Lt Cooper, the pilot, was known as an individual who would not permit any infraction of flying regulations. He conducted his operations, at all times, in accordance with Army Air Force rules and regulations. Lt. Cooper had a total of 1172:15 hours, of which 77:35 was in the B-29, Lt. Eslinger, the co-pilot, had a total of 658:50 of which 96:45 was B-29 time and of this 89:20 was co-pilot time. Both men were considered good pilots. Now, 2 hours and 9 minutes after taking off from Walker Army Air Force Base the B-29 was on the path to destruction. They had flown low across Copeland, slowly descending; started a right turn and one half-mile south of the town dragged a wing. Immediately the wing burst into flame.

On this 17 September 1944 Sunday evening it was quiet and calm at the 0. H. Hatfield residence. Mr. Hatfield, called "Hat" by his friends was an old timer in the area. He had built the home, the barn, and other out buildings, on the farm, with his own hands. He had also built many buildings in the farming community of Gray County, Kansas. He had represented Gray County in the Kansas legislature, had large farming interests, and was chairman of the Gray County Republican Central Committee. He was a respected and loved member of the community.

Mrs. Kittie Hatfield, 0. H. Hatfield's wife, and his daughter Ruth Evelyn Settles were in the dining room with him. Ruth Settles was married to Captain Orice Dean Settles, and living with her parents while her husband was overseas. Her baby son, Jay Dean Settles, was asleep upstairs in his crib. Captain Settles had recently spent a 30-day leave with his wife; getting acquainted with his baby son. When Captain Settles had returned to his overseas post, Mrs Settles and the baby had accompanied him to New York. They had just returned.

0. H. Hatfield was seated at his desk, his wife and daughter setting at the dining room table when the roar of four giant engines on the B-29 shattered the quiet Sunday evening calm. Mr. Hatfield raised his head from his work, and in a calm voice said, "that fellow is flying pretty low."

When the wing of the B29 struck the ground, in the shallow right turn, immediately started burning and turned in a westerly direction. It continued another 150 yards and slammed into the lonely 0. H.

Hatfield farmhouse. It totally disintegrated and burned the farmhouse, barn, and other outbuildings. The ten-man crew, O. H. Hatfield, and the baby, Jay Dean Settles, were killed instantly. God only knows what thoughts went through the minds of Lt. Wayne B. Cooper, the pilot, and Lt. Lawrence H. Eslinger when the right wing hit the ground and they realized they were to low. There was no explosion. The plane tore itself apart hitting the ground.

There was a horrible fire. The farm gas tank contained 600 gallons, and the plane probably had about 3500 gallons remaining. Everything burned 9,000 tons of wheat in the barn that had just been harvested, and all the equipment. The only thing left was the walls of a stone garage standing stark and alone, completely gutted.

A passing motorist found Ruth Settles, and Kittie Hatfield in the yard, dazed, bruised, bleeding and burned. He took them to the Hospital in Dodge City, Kansas. They were severely injured, and they were a long time in recovery. It was a miracle they survived. Many people from Copeland came to help, including the congregation of the Copeland Methodist Church, and the Reverend Marshall R. Hinds.

The United States Army Air Corp moved in the next day. A team of investigators started checking on the cause of the accident. They searched out people in Copeland who had seen the low flying aircraft go over the town. They measured and calculated every aspect of the crash searching for a cause. Hand written notes were made, and a complete hand written report was prepared by September 20, 1944. Part of that report reads as follows:

"The aircraft was spread over an area of approximately one-half mile in length and two hundred yards in width. Three of the engines continued three hundred fifty yards beyond the main part of the wreckage, while the fourth engine continued one hundred eighty yards beyond there.

Marks on the ground indicated that the airplane was in a turn to the right, and the blades of the No. 4 propeller struck the ground first."

On September 18, 1944, in the hand written notes was the following surprising bit of information:

"Co pilot was friend of Capt. Settles, husband of injured woman, son-in-law of Mr. Hatfield, who was killed. Co pilots aunt and uncle lived in Copeland, Mr. Sterling Somerville. He was refuted on a previous occasion to have buzzed Copeland."

"THE JACKSONIAN" newspaper from Cimarron, Kansas wrote the following about Lt. Eslinger:

"Morning revealed that the destroyed bomber was a B-29 Superfortress. It was soon established that the pilot of the plane was not the stranger for whom the village had felt that abstract sorrow felt for fellow-man regardless of acquaintanceship. Walker Army Air Field near Hays, (Ks.) reported him as a lad that had spent so many summers here that he seemed one off our lads. He was Lt. Lawrence Eslinger, nephew of Mrs. V. E. Reese, and Sam and Sterling

Somerville, all Copeland residents.

Lawrence was the son of Mr. and Mrs. Harold Eslinger, now of Manhatten. Until a few years ago they had resided at Kinsley where the Hatfields, also pioneer Kinsley residents, had been their neighbors. During his high school and college years Lawrence had spent most of his summers at Copeland, and for a time was employed at the Hatfield farm. He entered into the church and community life of Copeland and his clear tenor voice, mingled with the rich bass of Dean Settles, the alto of Ruth Hatfield (now Mrs. Settles) and the soprano of Jean Emmons Koeling formed a quartette that will always be remembered by Copeland people."

The October 5, 1944 issue of "THE JACKSONIAN" reported that Captain Dean Settles had arrived home:
"Capt. Dean Settles arrived home from England Wednesday after getting word of the death of his son Jay Dean and his father-in-law, 0. H. Hatfield. He had been recently sent back to England and was there a week when he received the word. He said he was just 2 days coming from Scotland to Great Bend, Kansas."

The house and farm buildings were never rebuilt, and after Mrs. Kittie Hatfield died her sister inherited the farm. Dean Settles, left the Air Force at the end of the war. Mrs Settles had recovered, and they farmed for a few years, and then went to Alaska. Dean Settles was a school principal for years and Mrs Settles was a music teacher and a librarian. They worked mainly in Anchorage, but did much work educating young people in remote areas of Alaska. Ty Settles, their son, told me the following in a letter:

Dad was active with the YMCA in Anchorage serving on its board for quite a while. Mom was active in music circles, and both were very active in youth activities. Dad and a couple other principals were responsible for the first organized hockey program in Anchorage, and mom was a cheerleading sponsor for a number of years at one of the high schools in the
Anchorage. They retired once, and moved to Colorado. They had been there only a few months when a friend of theirs, who was a superintendent of a bush school district called... a principal and a teacher had left town in the middle of winter without telling anyone they weren't coming back. So the folks went back up for two or three years to a small Indian village on the Yukon river and finished their careers in a place called Tanana, Alaska."

The accident report consists of 117 pages of reports, letters, statements, and conclusions. There was no reason for the low altitude of the plane over Copeland, which was *750* feet higher than Walker Air Force Base, and the fact he had his landing lights on ruled out the pilot unknowingly flying into the ground. Much stress was made of the co-pilot's association within the town of Copeland: *"It would certainly appear that flight over that town was other than coincidence."* The fact that Lt. Weber (the navigator who was removed from the plane due to illness) testified that the crew had flown over Copeland on a previous occasion pointed out an individual personal interest in that location.

Lt Cooper, the pilot, was pictured as not the type of individual to permit any infraction of flying regulations, and at all times conducted his operations in accordance with all the rules and regulations.

Col. William C. Cain, President; Major Floyd E. Wikstrom, member; and 1st Lt. Eugene W. Schrage, accident investigation made the final decision. They determined, in their Decision of The Board, that the accident was caused by intentional low flying, and the responsibility for the accident lies with the airplane commander, 2nd Lt. W. B. Cooper.

BROTHERS

After the five Sullivan brothers, from Iowa, were all killed on the same ship early in WW1 1, the War Department made every effort to separate brothers, and especially not allow them to serve in the same units. One exception was Alton F. Pierce and Ted B. Pierce from East Hartford, Coin, of the 390th Bomb Group. They flew in combat with the 390 Bomb Group, on the same crew, for a total of 34 out of 35 missions.

Al was the oldest. He was born June 18, 1923 and Ted was born June 13, 1924 in Cape Cod, Mass. They enlisted in the Air Force together on March 2, 1943 took basic together, and went to gunnery school at Buckinghan field, Fort Myers, Florida. Upon completing gunnery training they were sent to Avon Field, Florida for phase training. Here they were assigned to a crew and practiced flying as a crew being made ready for combat.

Here at Avon Field, Florida, for the first time Al found his name taken off the crew that Ted was assigned to. Al hurried down and talked to the person who made up the crew lists, who said there was nothing he could do, "orders are orders." Al, not to be deterred, went to the chaplain who told him he didn't think it possible to have them put on the same crew. However in a couple days Al found himself assigned to the same crew as Ted. They later learned that their parents had been contacted for permission to assign them to the same crew.

They flew together for 34 out of their 35 missions. Al was a T/Sgt. Top turret gunner and engineer, and Ted (slightly wounded in the right leg on the third mission) was a S/Sgt. Right waist gunner and assistant engineer. The crew was a tight knit group, and several of them flew all their missions together. Their pilot was George H. McKee.

When they returned to the United States they were assigned to gunnery instructors school, and finished the war at a gunnery school in Arizona. They were discharged together in October 1945.

The determination, love and loyalty of the Pierce brothers to stick together, in spite of most commanding officers wanting to split them up, is an emotional heart warming story. It carried over into civilian life and they still live near each other, Al in Storrs, Conn and Ted in Coventry, Conn.

Front l to r:
D.G. Grant (CP); G.H. McKee (P); M.H. Banner (N)

Standing:
A.F. Pierce (E),; V.L. Miller (TG); F.A. Sparacino (BT); T.B. Pierce (WG); J.A. Delaloye (RO)

AIR SEA RESCUE MISSION
APRIL 19, 1944

One of the advantages of being an inexperienced crew, who survived the Schweinfurt mission, kept us out of combat for 6 days. There was a mission scheduled for today to Kassel, Germany, but we were assigned an air sea rescue mission to look for an English airman who was down in the North Sea We were awakened at 3:30 AM, had breakfast, drew our flight gear, and were briefed to fly to an English AB and they would brief us on the search pattern we were to perform.

All this sounded fine but there was a thick layer of fog hanging over Grafton Underwood. At 5:00 AM we took off, and soon climbed out of the fog. It looked like all of England was involved with The bad weather, but after flying our assigned course for a few minutes ahead and to our right we saw a searchlight probing the sky. This identified the field we were to land ~but the fog was fill lying on the ground as we could see from the searchlight. We called the airfield and asked for landing instructions, and a big circle of lights came on. We had been briefed on this and were to fly round the circle of lights and be led into a funnel marking the runway lights in fog are easy to see when you are directly overhead and the funnel lined us up with the runway, and at 500 feet, as we started our approach here was a red, amber and green light ahead of us, By holding the airplane on the green light and the funnel narrowing we descended right to the runway. If you got in the amber light you ware getting low, and the red light was danger, you are much to low. At about 50 feet we saw the runway, and made a landing.

The British treated us like royalty, gave us coffee, and showed us on a map of the area we were to search. It was way up in the North Sea, a couple hundred miles from the Coast of Denmark. Denmark had German fighters based there plus the fighter bases in the Netherlands and Germany. They advised the gunners to stay alert. We were looking for a single man in a dinghy, and prayed we would find him.

The fog was starting to lift when we took off and the mission scheduled for today was completed in spite of the weather. We picked up our course, and started out over the North Sea, dark and foreboding. Lt Aldo Rovero, the navigator, kept us on course and took us to our assigned area. We then started flying a grid at about 100 feet off the water, everyman with his eyes glued to the cold rough waves beneath us.

Flying over water at a low altitude is deceptive. You loose your depth perception, and suddenly need the copilot to fly. If he's been staring at the water for a long time he needs you to fly. We alternated, and watched the instruments when we weren't flying.

Our mission was unsuccessful. We flew 8 hours and 30 minutes, and didn't see a thing, not even another airplane. We were very happy the Germans didn't send fighters to investigate our activities. It was along hard lonesome day and I hope the Englishman knew, before he died, that someone was looking for him. It was a depressing day, and it was a tired disgusted crew that returned to Grafton Underwood.

We flew in B-17 42-237792 JD-B, "Bermondsey." She was accepted by the U.S. Army Air Force August 30, 1943, and was assigned overseas on October 10, 1943. She ns sent to the 305th Bomb Group November 2, 1943. In November of 1943 she was assigned to Base Air Depot #1 at Burtonwood and returned to the Group on Novetnber 10. 1943. On February, 1944 she was assigned to 2 Strategic Air Depot, AE Little Staughton and AF Abbots Ripton. She was returned to the Group February 7,1944. On July16, 1944 she was sent to the 487th Bomb Group.

High Profile Prisoners of War

The Story of John G Winant, Jr.

John G. Winant, Jr. was a student at Princeton University when the Japanese attacked Pearl Harbor. He would have graduated in 1945, His dad who, had flown in the Eighth Observation Squadron in WW 1, was a high official in the Roosevelt Administration could have kept him out of combat.

John, Jr. however, quit college, enlisted in the Aviation Cadet Program and received his wings in September of 1942. He was an original member of the 390th Bomb Group and flew his B-17 to England.

His father had been appointed Ambassador to Great Britton, and John Jr. was able to meet his mother and father in London.
After a month in England attending ground school and flying practice formations he missed the first mission because his plane wasn't ready.

On August 17, 1943 John and his crew took part in the Regensburg, Germany mission flying across Germany, the Mediterranean, landing in North Africa. This was the third mission for the Group. Jon and his crew flew 12 missions, and on October 10, 1943 they were shot down on the terrible Munster, Germany mission. It was the 22nd mission for the Group, and John U. Winant, Jr's thirteenth mission.

Captain James Geary was flying the lead plane on this mission, "Pistol Packin' Mama" and saw Winant's plane explode, and only a few chutes come out of the explosion. Captain Geary landed at Thorpes Abbott, home of the 100th Bomb Group. When he returned to Framlingham he received a phone call from the Ambassador to England, John U. Winant Senior asking what were his son's chances.

Capt. Geary told him that anything was possible, but, keeping it to himself, thought it not probable.

Captain James Geary decided to fly a second tour, and transferred to the 100 Bomb Group. He was shot down on a mission to Berlin in early 1944. When Capt. Geary reached the POW camp at Sagan the first person he ran into was Lt. John G. Winant, Jr.

The crew flying with Lt. Winant, Jr that day consisted of the following:

Pilot	Lt. John G. Winant, Jr	POW
CP	Lt Donald C. Arns	POW
N	Lt. Robert A. Tredinnick	POW
B	Lt. Richard E. Walker	POW
E	T/S Walter Weidemain	POW
R	T/S Paul E. Hurles	KIA
BT	S/S Elmer Fjosne	KIA
WG	S/S Robert V. Wirtz	KIA
WG	S/S Alonzo J. Swope	POW
TG	S/S Frank M. Malone	KIA

I mention the crew names, because the names of those who were killed In Action should never be forgotten.

In mid 1944 Lt. Winant, was transferred from Stalag Luff III in Sagen to Oflag IVC, Colditz Castle near Leipzig in eastern Germany. It was a forbidding place. High cold stone walls and towers. The Germans considered it escape proof so they brought people there who constantly tried to escape. Lt. John G. Winant, Jr was the only 390th POW to be imprisoned at Colditz. When he walked through the massive doors of the castle he immediately became a "Very Important Prisoner." The Germans could use him as a hostage or for ransom, and he was in very important company.

There was Giles Romilly, Churchill's nephew; Charles Hopetown, son of the Viceroy to India, Lord Linlithgow; Captain John

Elphinstone, nephew of the Queen; Lt. Viscount George Lascelles, the Kings nephew; Captain Dawyer Haig, son of Britain's WW1 Field Marshall.

There was a Polish General Bor Kumoronski and 16 prominent Polish Prisoners, and four French Generals. Lt John G. Winant, Jr was the only American in the group.

On April 12, 1945 when Colditz was in danger of being over run by American Forces, the SS took control of the English and American VIP prisoners, and started moving them to Southern Germany. It was known at the time that the SS had fortified an area in the mountains of Southern Germany. It was to be used by Hitler, and other high ranking members of the Nazi party at the end of the war. However as the war ended some high ranking SS officers seeking to gain favor turned the VIP prisoners over to the Swiss Government. The ordeal was over.

John G. Winant, Jr came home and finished college. He was a stock broker during his life, and died in 1994 of a heart attack.

As a side light, Stars and Stripes carried an article dated Oct. 19, 1943 that the son of Ambassador Winant was a POW of the Germans.
"Probably more pleased than anybody however was Sgt E. M Clark of Flies burg Wash., who packed Winant 's parachute before he took off "I'm glad his chute opened," Clark said. "It sorta makes you feel like your doing something worthwhile."

SMOKESTACK LEADER, SLOW DOWN?

The sky over Oberpfafferihofen, Germany dawned bright and clear, on the morning of April 24, 1944. At 20,000 feet it was cloudless, frigid cold, a bright blue and empty. Birds didn't venture to this altitude. There was nothing to spoil the tranquility, and there was no hint of the terrible battle that was to be fought there later in the day. The peaceful sky would be riddled with screaming shrapnel snarling 20 mm and 50 caliber machine gun slugs, black greasy flak bursts, parts of heavy bombers, and fighters would fall to the ground, along with the dangling bodies hanging from parachutes.

Early that morning crews of the 8thAir Force were preparing for a mission to bomb the Dorner-Werke GmbH Factory and Airfield. Being built here was the Do-335 MehrzweckJagdflugzeug (Multipurpose Fighter Aircraft). The Do-335 was powered by two DB-603 As or 603-Fs engines, both housed in the fuselage. The front engine drove a tractor propeller in the nose, and the rear engine drove a pusher propeller installed behind the tail unit. The Do-335 was developed in nine months, and had its first flight on October 28, 1943. It was a unique design and is important because it is still considered the world's fastest piston powered aircraft. Though it was still in the development stage, the Luftwaffe expected it to become a first line fighter. Because of the efforts like the April 24, 1944 mission by many brave young men, only 40 of these aircraft were built.

The mission was plagued with troublesome problems, some questionable judgments, and incidents of high heroism. It was considered important enough to win for the 384th Bombardment Group the Distinguished Unit Citation.

It all began with the Field Order coming in on the teleprinter at about 2300 April 24, 1944. Charles Bishop, who did this for many months at headquarters, started taking the mission for Station 106, the 384th Bombardment Group came alive with preparations to "Get

The Show On The Road." Squadrons started putting the crews together, Engineering Officers started counting the available planes, Crew Chiefs ran engines at full power, testing the output and making last minute adjustments. Crew Chiefs and their crews could look forward to some sleep if their plane was selected for the mission. Cooks started breakfast, intelligence prepared for briefing the crews, and armament loaded bombs and ammunition. The planes were loaded with gasoline and oil.

Colonel Dale 0. Smith, Commanding Officer of the 384th Bomb Group, was called about 2400 hours and made aware that a mission was on. General Robert Travis, Commanding Officer of the 41st Combat Wing, 1st Division, would be leading the 41st "A" Combat Wing, arid that he, Colonel Smith, would be leading the 41st "B" Combat Wing. It would be a maximum effort with the 384th putting up 30 aircraft.

Brigadier General Robert Falligant Travis was born in Savannah, Georgia, on December 26, 1904. He was graduated from the US. Military Academy at West Point, N. Y. and commissioned a Second Lieutenant of Field Artillery June 9, 1928. The following September he entered the Air Corp Primary Flying School at Brooks Field, Texas. Upon completion of the course, he transferred to the Air Corp Advanced Flying School at Kelly Field, Texas, from which he was graduated with the rating of Pilot in September 1929.

Colonel Dale 0. Smith was born in Reno, on March 7,1911. He attended Reno Schools and the University of Nevada, being there for two years before being appointed to the United States Military Academy. He graduated from West Point in 1934 and spent the summer on a Midshipmen Cruise to Europe aboard the battle-ship "Wyoming." Returning to the United States he went to flying school at Randolph and Kelly Fields, Texas.

The mission was all spelled out in the Field Order. It left nothing to the imagination. On this day however, there was an ominous notation that was going to spell disaster for many crews of the 384th 303rd, and the 306th Bombardment Groups. It was written down in the Field Order, and it had been dreamed up by the staff of General "One Eye" Willie Williams, Commanding Officer of the 8th Air Force 1st Division Headquarters.

The normal Composition of Force (the line up of Combat Wings going into enemy territory) was given. There would be five Combat Wings the 41st "A", the 41st "B", the 40th, the 1st, and the 94th bringing up the rear. Each Combat Wing was made up of three Groups of 18 to 21 planes. Normally the Combat Wings would have gone into enemy territory in a bomber stream with 4 to 6 miles between each Combat Wing that would contain 54 to 63 heavy bombers. We would have gone into enemy territory just as indicated in the Composition of Force 41 "A", 41 "B", 40th, 1st and 94th.

The ominous notation on this Field Order was just below the Composition of Force and said:
"41st 'B' will guide left on 41 'A'."
"1st will guide right on 40th"

This simple notation spelled trouble for the 1st Division, and for the 41st "B" Combat Wing in particular. It was a deadly serious order, and because of it, brave young men would die, or become prisoners of war. It would reflect on the leadership of General Robert Travis, and Colonel Dale 0. Smith, both West Pointers; Smokestack Leader, and Smokestack Blue Leader respectively.

For the first time instead of a bomber stream we would be going into enemy territory in two Combat Wings abreast or in echelon. The 41st "A" to the left and slightly ahead of the 41st "B".

Behind us the 1st and 49th Combat Wings are in echelon and the 94th would be bring up the rear alone. This then was the baffle order of the 1st Division.

The 41st "A" Combat Wing was made up of two Groups, the 379th and the 303rd. General Robert Travis, as stated, led this Wing. His call sign was Smokestack Leader.

The 41st "B" Combat Wing was made up of all 384th planes in the lead group. All 306th planes in the low group, and the high group consisted of 2 Squadrons of 384th planes, and 1 Squadron (seven planes) from the 303rd Bomb Group. Colonel Dale 0. Smith led the 41st "B" Combat Wing and his call sign was Smokestack Blue.

We staggered through the darkness and stumbled down the black wet road to the mess hall. We had unceremoniously been hustled out of the sack and told we were on for the day. Apprehensive and worried about the horrors the day would bring we found the fresh eggs for breakfast unpalatable. Still nervous through the briefing, the fear factor increased upon seeing the string stretched deep into Germany. After checking out the day's flight gear we were finally hauled out to our airplane; in my case B-17G, number 430(42-102430). Once in the cockpit, busy with the checklist; starting the engines things settled down. All we had to do now was taxi out at the proper time, and to take off 30 seconds after the plane ahead of us.

Taxi time was 0835, and Lt. Boger was 1st off at 0854. Smokestack Blue leader was late in getting off the ground, due to trouble with his airplane. He was off at 0906 hours in B-17 C, 42-38014, and immediately started forming up his Group. All 30 planes were off the ground by 0934 hours, Station 106, Grafton Underwood. returned to normal daytime activities,

After take off, our Squadron Leader started a slow turn to the left, and my job was to catch hint I would then fall into the number 6 spot in the low squadron of 7 planes in the high group. It was up to Squadron Leader to find the group of 20 airplanes, and up to the Group Leader to find the Combat Wing of 54 to 63 airplanes.

Airborne in squadron formation the radio comes alive with calls of, "Where are you?" Some one in and angry voice exclaims, "Slow down!" Smokestack Blue Leader at 0930 hours came on the radio with, "Smokestack Blue Leader to all ships: Please observe VHF discipline, no unnecessary transmissions. 251, close it up."

It all came together. Squadrons formed up, then groups, until we were a large unwieldy group of about 58 planes flying in Combat Wing formation. From here until the end of the mission, the pilots the pilots were intently focused on, and concentrating on holding their position in the formation. The crew is in position except the ball turret gunner who will get in the ball over the channel before we enter enemy territory.

We departed the English coast (Beachy Head) 1100 hours at 15,300 feet At Beachy Head we changed course approximately 40 degrees to the right. This was a change to the right and had no effect on our position because 41 "B" was on the inside of the turn. If anything it tended to pull us up even with the lead 41 "A" Group. We crossed the French Coast at 1118 hours at 18,300 feet, and came back to a heading of approximately 113 degrees. This was a 39-degree change in heading and it was to the left. Being on the outside of the turn our leader had to speed up to hold his position on 41 "A". This left those planes in the back of the formation out of position, left behind by the turn and starting to play "catch up" by increasing their airspeed. As our leader increased his airspeed to regain his position on the 41st "A" Combat Wing, the heavily loaded planes in the 41st "B" Combat Wing fell further and further behind,.

At 1123 hours, just after crossing the enemy coast a 306th Bombardment Group aircraft 42-31445 was hit by flak. The pilot, Lt. Peterson, pulled out of formation, flames coming from his number 4 engine. Parachutes started coming out, and about a minute later the plane blew up. Three or four chutes were seen to have opened.

The cussing and shouting started over the radio, as exasperated pilots struggled to keep up and stay in formation.. "Smokestack Blue Leader, slow down," they shouted with some expletives thrown in. This infuriated Smokestack Blue Leader, but there wasn't much he could do about it. However, this was a good indication that 41 "B" was in trouble on turns to the left. It was like kids playing crack-the-whip. On turns to the left Smokestack Blue Leader increased his speed, and caused the formation to spread out and straggle.

It also became apparent that wiser heads were leading the 40th Combat Wing and the 1st Combat Wing. They were supposed to be in echelon formation the same as 41 "A" and 41 "B". Because of the problem in the turns they had taken an inline position in the bomber stream. They had discarded the echelon formation and were flying inline behind 41 "A" with a 4 mile interval between Combat Wings. The 94th Combat Wing brought up the rear. Now only 41 "B" was in echelon on 41 "A", outside the bomber stream to the right. We were all alone out there. We were trailed off and dispersed; fighting to stay in formation; straining our engines; sweating and cussing to keep up. We were setting ducks of any German fighters looking for and easy Group, or better yet a Combat Wing.

In a report on Planning, Execution, and Results of Mission to Oberpfaffenhofen, Germany, April 24, 1944, directed to the Commanding Officer of the 40th Combat Wing (H) AAF, APO 557 is the following paragraph:
"306th Bomb Group, low in the 41st 'B' Combat Wing: All A/C took off on time and made a normal assembly over Molesworth. The lead group departed Molesworth on time with groups in Combat Wing formation. Route over England was as briefed, departing Beachy Head on time and on course. Some difficulty in alignment of the Combat Wings was encountered and the 41st 'B' Combat Wing was to the right and rear, flying alone throughout the mission. The low group of this wing was further forced out of position due to a straggling low squadron in the lead group....

Leading the straggling low squadron that forced the 306th low group out of position was Lt. Walter F. (Big Dog) Harvey in aircraft 42-31346. Lt. Harvey was leading the low squadron (544th) of the lead 384th Group of the 41st "B" Combat Wing. Lt. Harvey had been checking out new crews for the 384th. He instructed them on what to expect in combat; checked the pilot out in a fully loaded B-l7, and flying missions with them until he felt the pilot capable. On this day, shortly after a normal takeoff, Lt. Harvey lost a supercharger on one engine. Aborting the mission was not in his nature, and he struggled on. He hoped that after he reached altitude, he could close it up and maintain his position in the formation.. Smokestack Blue Leader radioed him to close it up, but he couldn't do it.

Forty miles east of Paris, with Lt. Harvey flying, aircraft 42-31346 received a direct burst of flak. For a few terrifying seconds the plane flew on as though nothing had happened then fire and smoke were seen in the cockpit. Four chutes were seen to emerge, and three were seen to have opened. The crew consisted of the following:

P.	1st Lt.	Harvey, Walter L.	EVD
CP.	2nd Lt.	Brown, Robert H.	EVD
N.	2nd Lt.	Rule, Johnson W.	EVD
B.	1st Lt	Rader, Richard E.	EVD
R.	S/Sgt.	Sturak, Stanley.	POW
TT.	S/Sgt.	Smith, Dewey C.	POW
BT.	Sgt.	Roberson, Charles W.	POW
TG.	Sgt.	Vann~ Charles D.	POW
WG.	Sgt	Atkins, James A.	EVD
WG.	Sgt.	McManus, Cornelius P.	EVD

Lt. Harvey and Lt. Dick Radar spent 15 or 16 weeks down behind enemy lines. They managed to evade the Germans, and after many close calls hooked up with an American scout outfit that was many miles behind the lines, and were returned to the 384th in August of 1944.

About 75 miles West of Paris at 1135 hours, 20,000 feet we turned to a heading of approximately 126 degrees, but this was a right turn that didn't change 41st "B"'s position. It did allow some trailing planes to close up on the formation. However, 100 miles East of Paris at 1158 hours, 20,000 feet, we made a 28 degree course change to the left. This correction to the left, caused our 41st "B" Combat Wing to fall miles behind 41 "A". We were behind the 40th Combat Wing in the bomber stream, but still off to the right and all alone.

To compound the problem Smokestack Blue Leader increased his indicated air speed, in an attempt to regain his position, and that further scattered our 41st "B" Combat Wing.

Those in the rear or the 41st "B" Combat Wing were left to struggle to catch up. There were no radio signals warning of the increase in speed, and a large formation of 60 airplanes is an unwieldy mass to slow down, to turn, and to speed up. There was a certain amount of lag, until you realized you were falling behind, and then you punished your engines to catch up. There were anonymous radio calls from the pilots, "G. . ..d…it, Smokestack Blue Leader, slow down." Cries of, "Slow down, slow down." Others more profane, and need not be repeated here, but on the same theme. "Smokestack Blue Leader, slow down." We were a scattered mess, and it would be an hour before we were a formation again.

South of Strasbourg at 1246 hours we changed course again. A 13 degree left turn effectively scattered us again when Smokestack Blue Leader speeded up to hold his position on Smokestack Leader's right. We were now well into Germany and our luck in coming across France without seeing enemy fighters, was about to change. No doubt German fighters had been vectored in on this strung-out Combat Wing. Stray fighter units that had seen us couldn't believe their eyes. Here was an entire Combat Wing, away from the main bomber stream, strung out and all alone; ripe to be plucked. German fighter proceeded to pluck the flock.

The first enemy attack came between 1215 and 1230 hours by Me-109s. This attack was driven off by six P-51s. The Me-109s with the P-51s following, dove through he 41st "B" high group. American and German guns were firing, but no bombers were seen to go down.

At 1319 hours passing north of Leipheim and southeast of Stuttgart, the roof fell in. Approaching the Augsburg area from 1219 hours until 1326 hours we were hit by 50 Me-109s and Fw109s coming in two, four, and eight abreast head on from 12 o'clock high. Some enemy fighters flew straight through squadrons and groups returning to the head of the formation and repeating the head-on attacks.

From 1319 hours until reaching the target at 1358 hours 41st "B" Combat Wing would be under unrelenting fighter attacks. Before the target was reached, sixteen B-I7s had been shot out of the 41st "B" Combat Wing, and the 306th didn't have any bombs left. The 41st "A" dispatched 58 bombers and lost zero. The 41st "B" lost those 16 bombers trying to maintain a position outside the bomber stream to the right and slightly behind 41st "A". Something had to be wrong in 41st "B" to attract the swarm of enemy fighters that inflicted such damage upon us.

Our leader certainly contributed to our misery. His hardheaded decision to stay in position on 41st "A", when the other groups had fallen into the bomber stream, left us alone on the out right side of the main force. The unexpected airspeed increases scattered our formation and left us vulnerable to the enemy fighters.

When their leader got in trouble, the 306th Bomb Group, low group in the 41st "B" Combat Wing, had followed him down to 14,000 feet, salvoed their bombs, and then returned to the Combat Wing. When we made the bomb run over the target the 306th Bomb Group didn't have any bombs.

General Travis was a proud man. In his tailor made uniforms, he was striking, and always reminded me of Errol Flynn. He was tall, with black hair, and handsome. He was not the type man to relinquish or give up his lead position in the charge to the target. It would have been very irritating to him had a Colonel passed him up on the bomb run, hut that's exactly what happened.

The map shows that our route to the target required an approximate 45-degree, 90-degree, and an 80-degree turn. All to the right, which caused the 41st "B" to close up and eventually, pass the 41st "A". This happened on the bomb rum, and Travis's language was rather profane on the radio. It was summed up best in the Operations Officer's Report to the Commanding Officer of the 379th Bomb Group for mission of April 24, 1944:

"Difficulty was encountered, particularly on the route in, with the air division assembly. Our lead aircraft cruised at 145 - 150 MPH in order to allow the combat wing guiding on the left to get into formation, which they never did. As a result this combat wing (41st 'B') passed over the target before the air division lead."

The 379th Group Leader's Narrative, Major William C. Sipes, Lead Group had this to say:
"As we were heading towards the IP (initial point) the other Combat Wing (41st 'B') did not take sufficient interval behind us and as a result they went over the target first. Proceeded on to the target. The weather was clear. No flak (I don't know where this guy was). Bombing results were good. Run was made on A.F.C E. (automatic pilot)."

The above fiasco would have been funny had not several B-I7s and their crew of 10 men been shot down. Brave young men died while our leaders jockeyed for position. Custer had led such a charge June 26th 1876.

Colonel Smith made no mention of his bombing first in his report. The "41st'B" Combat Wing Commander's Narrative of Mission

Flown on April 24, 1944:

"Extreme difficulty was encountered guiding left on 41st 'A' Combat Wing as they made numerous turns which could not be previously determined, and on each turn distance was lost by 41st 'B' Combat Wing. We entered the enemy coast at 1118 hours, 49 degrees 55' N.- 00 degrees 56' E., 18,300 feet. In an effort to catch 41st 'A' Combat Wing, excessive speeds were used over France and this contributed to stringing out the wing formation. Prior to the target, flak encountered was moderate to intense generally, and accurate. Just prior to the IP, which was reached at 1351 hours, at 20,000 feet, we were abreast 41st 'A' Combat Wing."

Colonel Smith reported that the bombing results were good. All the aircraft in his group carried 500-pound general-purpose bombs. The 306th had no bombs, and the composite high group had maximum 47 A1s (incendiaries). The lead group dropped their 500-pound bombs on the target area. The three large buildings of the Aircraft Assembly Plant received direct hits. There was one certain and one probable on the northernmost of these buildings, at least three direct hits on the central building which was the MPI (maximum point of impact) and at least five direct hits on the eastern building. A smaller building in the northern part of the factory area received a direct hit. About one-fifth of the pattern was on the landing area. The high group dropped their M47 incendiaries in some woods and fields east of the airfield and the 306th had no bombs to drop.

SUMMARY AND CONCLUSION

Every member of the 384th Bombardment Group is entitled to the Distinguished Unit Citation with an Oak Leaf Cluster. One of these awards was won on April 24, 1944 on the Oberpfaffenhofen, Germany mission. Sixteen B-17s were lost, seven from the 33~]th Bomb Group, making a total of 20 planes lost in the month of April. This was the most losses in the 1st Division during any month of the war. When the 100th Bomb Group, third Division, lost 21 planes in one month they picked up the name, "Bloody Hundreth." The 384th was more fortunate, and came out of that disastrous month without a "Bloody" something being attached to her name and reputation.

Thirty-seven brave and honorable young men gave up their lives, and a record 13 heavy bombers went to Switzerland on this day.

It was not the intention of the *writer* to question the courage 01 General Robert Travis, and Colonel Dale 0. Smith. They were brave and honorable men. However, I can and do question their judgment in holding the 41st "B" out to the right of the bomber stream, when we were getting the hell kicked out of us. The man deserving the Silver Star that day was Captain Robert Langlois who held his burning airplane straight and level over the target, and did not leave until bombs were away.

There were other heros on this mission. There were pilots who brought crippled planes hack to Grafton Underwood, gunners who shot down enemy planes and never got credit for it. There were crewmen who saved a buddy's life with a walk-around oxygen bottle, or tended a wounded man. There were gunners who remained at their station, without ammunition, hut still tracking the enemy fighters.

Most of the German Luftwaffe fighters stationed in the west took a crack at us. They had time to attack, land and refuel, and come charging back. They were aggressive, and seemed intent on shooting down as many as they could. It was a day I have never forgotten, as I'm sure many others who were on this mission will carry the memory to their grave.

The 1st, 2nd, and 3rd Divisions of the 8th Air Force dispatched 754 heavy bombers on April 24, 1944 to targets at Oberpfaffenhofen, Landsberg, Erding, Leidheim, Gablingen and Fredrichahafen. The Air Force lost a total of 40 heavy bombers for the day. THE 41st "B" COMBAT WING SUFFERED 40 PER CENT OF THOSE LOSSFS.

The Bennett Crew

This photo take 6-21-44 after a mission to Berlin, Germany. Standing left to right: 1st Lt. Dewayne Bennett, pilot; Major George H. Koehne, Jr, co-pilot, air commander; 2nd Lt. Eugene E. Burcham, bombardier, 2nd Lt. William F. Kane, navigator; 2nd Lt. Howard W. Kell, tail gunner, observer. Kneeling left to right: S/Sgt. James D. Trumbo, waist gunner; T/Sgt. James A Holland, top turret gunner; S/Sgt. Verlin C. Gale, waist gunner; T/Sgt. Michael J. Perrone, radio; S/Sgt. Bernard Zelazoski; ball turret gunner.

Reunion

The Bennett crew St. Louis reunion 2000

Left to right:

Dwayne "Ben" Bennett. Venlin Gace, Tom Holland, Bernard Zelozoski and Paul Spiers

Official Mission Records of Dwayne Bennett

INDIVIDUAL SORTIE RECORD
(PAGE II)

#	DATE	TARGET	TIME	ROUNDS	E/A DESTROYED
1	4-10-44	Brussels/Evere			
2	4-11-44	Sorau			
3	4-13-44	Schweinfurt			
4	4-20-44	Sottievast			
5	4-22-44	Hamm			
6	4-24-44	Oberpfoffenhofen			
7	5-7-44	Berlin			
8	5-8-44	Berlin			
9	5-9-44	Thionville			
10	5-11-44	Saarbrucken			
11	5-13-44	Stettin			
12	5-15-44	Mimoyecques			
13	5-19-44	Berlin			
14	5-23-44	Nancy/Essey			
15	5-25-44	Sarreguemines			
16	5-29-44	Krzesinki			
17	5-30-44	Halberstadt			
18	6-5-44	La Pesse			
19	6-6-44	Meauvaines			
20	6-8-44	Orleans			
21	6-13-44	Dreux			
22	6-15-44	La Possenniere			
23	6-16-44	Laon/Athes			
24	6-21-44	Berlin			
25	6-24-44	Bremen			
26	6-25-44	Sens			
27	7-6-44	Vitry/En/Artois			

INDIVIDUAL SORTIE RECORD
(PAGE III)

	DATE	TARGET	TONNES	E/A DESTROYED
28	7-17-44	Eu		
29	7-19-44	Hollriegelsereuth		
30	8-1-44	Chartres		
31	8-3-44	Fiefs		
32				
33				
34				
35				
36				
37				
38				
39				
40				

I hereby certify that the above is a true record of the sorties accomplished by _____ while a member of the 384th Bombardment Group (H), AAF, in the European Theater of Operations.

A TRUE COPY

J. R. WYATT,
1st Lt., Air Corps,
Asst. Adjutant.